MW00527705

# Golf's

# Pace of Play

# Bible

## A Practical Guide and Plan for Improving Golf's Pace of Play

### And the

### Science Behind It

## Lucius Riccio Ph.D.

www.three45golf.org

ISBN: 0615889670
ISBN-13: 978-0615889672

Cover Photo by Eva Riccio

LUCIUS RICCIO

# CONTENTS

Preface     vii

1   Golf at a Crisis Point     1

2   The Problem Defined     7

     Time to Play 18 Holes

     Waiting Time to Hit

     Revenue Management

     Conclusion

3   Suggested Ways to Speed Up Play     13

4   Factory Physics     16

5   Previous Studies of Pace     26

6   Models of Pace of Play     29

     Single Group/Single Hole

     Single Group Bottleneck Analysis Model

     18 Hole/Multiple Group Simulation/Deterministic Times

     All Groups Playing at Same Pace

         Tee Interval Comparison

         Walking Speed Comparison

     Combination of Fast and Slow Groups

         Walking Speed Variation

Walking Speed/ Tight Tee Interval

Stroke Preparation/Hitting Pace

Tee Interval/Slow Hitting and Clearing

Slow Hitting and Clearing

18 Hole Bottleneck Analysis with Variable Times

Where Is The Bottleneck?

The Nature of the Course

Pace of Play, Tee Interval, and Revenue Management

7    The Plan: Bringing Back the 4 Hour Round        77

8    Tee Intervals                                    81

9    Course Set Up and Pace Management                85

10   Player and Group Behaviors                       93

11   Some Adjustment to the Rules of Golf             102

12   Implementing the Plan                            104

The Role of Psychology/The Role of Leadership

The Call to Arms

13   The Future                                       113

Concluding Unscientific Postscripts                  115

# PREFACE

Pace of Play has received a lot of attention recently. The USGA, the Golf Channel, the PGA of America, the American Junior Golf association and the NCAA to name just a few, have all made commitments to try to improve the time it takes to play a round of golf.

There is a reason for this interest: the time to play 18 holes of golf has gotten to the point of being intolerable and a threat to the health and growth of the game. Have you not noticed? Perhaps you are new to the game and think that 5 hour rounds are normal. Perhaps like millions of others, you have left the game or play far less. But for those of us who remember when it took less than 4 hours to play, who love the game, who want to play as much as we can, and who want to see the game grow and prosper, something has to be done to correct the situation.

My favorite philosopher is Yogi Berra. He once said "you know, you can observe a lot, just by watching." How do people learn the Rules of Golf? Probably not one in one hundred have even seen a Rules Book. Probably not one in 10,000 knows there is a big book of Decisions on the Rules of Golf. So how do we learn? We learn by watching and asking the people around us.

How do we learn about Pace of Play? Unfortunately, we learn our pace habits the same way. Most of the time, we learn by watching bad habits, habits which have been ingrained over long periods of time. Some are the result of frustration ("Why speed up? We'll just wait on the next tee."), and some from watching the pros on TV take two minutes to putt. We need to break those habits and change the way people think about pace of play.

The idea behind this book and the Three/45 Golf Association is to provide a solution to the problem by creating a sustained, long term presence for the issue, to serve as an organization of advocates for a more enjoyable approach to the game, to educate everyone associated with the game on the complexity of the problem and the principles which can lead to a quicker pace of play, to promote and disseminate research, and most importantly to create and advance a Plan and a set of Principles which when implemented will make the game better. The issue needs leadership, and I believe that leadership will come from every golfer who is concerned about the health of the game and the enjoyment it provides.

Campaigns are good. But when the campaign is over and the problem has not been solved, people get frustrated and return to their old habits. This issue comes and goes in the media and in the general discussion. It surfaces every now and then. People agree it is a problem, but when progress is not made, golfers tire of it and return to their old habits.

Suggestions as to how to speed up play which on the surface may sound good but are just one part of this complex problem, just lead to more frustration. A comprehensive science of pace of play is needed and a comprehensive plan of what everyone in the game must do needs to be offered before there is any hope of making a real dent in this problem. This book is an effort at providing both.

The Pace of Play problem can be solved. It should NOT be thought of like the weather, of which people can talk about but do nothing to affect it. For pace of play, we CAN do something about it.

It will not be easy to make improvements. Since it is a complex issue, it will take everyone involved in golf to cooperate. By reading this book, you have made a significant first step to help the game of golf. I hope, after you read this book, you will join the movement for a quicker pace of play and make a commitment to become an advocate and a leader.

LUCIUS RICCIO

# 1 GOLF AT A CRISIS POINT

The Game of Golf in America is at a crisis point. The growth of the game has stopped, by some measures it has declined. There are 3 million fewer golfers today in America than just a decade ago. Rounds played are down by 10%, although there has been some recent improvement in that statistic.

Golf is a big business in America. People watch football, watch baseball, watch basketball. People *play* golf. Golf is driven by people *playing the game*, not just watching it. Approximately 25 million Americans identify themselves as regular golfers. The industry generates $85 billion a year of economic activity, placing it ahead of the motion picture industry in GDP contribution. But that contribution has not kept up with the growth of the national economy.

A historical perspective is helpful. Growth of the game in America was steady from its introduction in the late 19th century all through the 20th century. Growth was so strong, the National Golf Foundation in 1988 published a report [1] that golf course development had lagged so significantly behind the growth in the interest for the game that it postulated that the country needed to open new golf courses at the rate of one new course per *day* for the next decade just to meet the demand.

Developers met that demand by building 3500 new courses in the decade of the '90s. However something unexpected happened. Toward the end of the century, growth in the number of rounds played leveled. In the past ten years little if any growth has been seen by operators of public and daily fee operators. And many private clubs have seen their waiting lists vanish. By the end of the first decade of this century the country experienced periods in which more golf courses were lost to other forms of development than new ones opened.

Although there are many reasons for this situation, one significant one is length of time it takes to play the game. Five and six hour rounds are not unheard of, forcing golfers to make a full day commitment to the sport each time they wish to play. The pressures of family and business make this an uncompetitive choice for far too many people.

The time it takes to play a round of golf at American golf courses is considered a major obstacle to the growth of the game, to increasing facility revenue and profitability, and to the enjoyment of the game for millions of golfers and would-be golfers. A study by Frank Thomas [2] found the time commitment to be the major barrier to people playing more golf. Many commentators have said similar things, and *no one complains that a round of golf takes too little time.*

There are at least three ways of looking at the growth problem. The drop in rounds could be the result of an unusually large drop in the number of people starting to play the game, an unusually large increase in the number giving up the game, and a significant drop in the number of rounds played by those still in the game. The drop in participation is likely a function of all three.

First it does seem that fewer people (particularly the young) are taking up the game. The PGA of America has started the Get Golf Ready program of inexpensive lessons. Jack Nicklaus has started a program to try to get more people (mostly kids) into the game using larger, easier to hit equipment. The First Tee is a great program to get young people involved. But these may not be enough. More programs have to be created to get more people into the game.

Second there is some truth to the notion that more than an unusual amount of golfers have stopped playing at all. Each year, some people leave the game, but in the past decade it seems more have dropped than the average amount. Part of that could be that the Baby Boom generation which populated the game in a big way in the 80s and 90s have grown old and drop out. But economic conditions (two recessions in the past decade) may be a big factor as well. The best businesses monitor "defections" and adjust their business models to keep customers from leaving. Every insurance salesman will tell you although finding new customers is important, keeping current customers is far more profitable.

The third is the amount of rounds played by those in the game. This seems to be a very big factor. The NGF estimates that the average number of rounds played per golfer has dropped by 10% in the past decade. Why? Time to play is likely a factor.

I founded the Three/45 Golf Association to combat this decline and to restore the time to play back to a reasonable length. The hope was that the organization could galvanize the concern into a meaningful movement, and with a critical mass of people supporting the principles behind a quicker pace, we could affect real change. Already almost all of the national golf organizations are either promoting progress directed at a quicker pace of play or preparing to launch efforts to encourage faster play. We, at the Three/45 Golf Association, see this as a positive trend. If it continues and as long as we do it right, don't get frustrated when we try and fail, and stay the course, progress can be made.

The Three/45 Golf Association's Pace of Play Principles ® are based on my research and the work of other concerned analysts, consultants and experts from various fields. A substantial amount of work has gone into the analysis of this problem. The one unfortunate thing I found was that since the problem is so complex and most analyses concentrate on only one or two of the multitude of competing issues which affect pace of play, the implementation of recommendations based on those studies have had limited success. I hope to bring all of that good work together into one strategy for correcting the problem.

This book is designed to provide a blueprint, a road map, a plan to improve the pace of play in America. It does that by taking advantage of a wide range of scientific studies, data collection efforts and real-world experiences. It recognizes the complexity of the problem but also points out practical, simple-to-understand principles which, when applied, can make a big difference in how long it takes to play the game and increase the enjoyment of all golfers.

# 2 PACE OF PLAY – THE PROBLEM DEFINED

There are several aspects to the problem of slow play depending on your point of view. For some the problem is that the overall time to finish a round is too long. For others long waiting periods before strokes can be played is the problem even if the overall time is not intolerable. For golf course operators, slow play may have an effect on the number of rounds they can provide (and sell) in a day.

There is some inter connectivity of these issues, but there is also some independence. There may even be some conflicts in that by improving one aspect, another may be hurt. Let's consider each one.

## Time to Play 18 Holes

The common wisdom is that the time it takes to play an 18 hole round has increased dramatically over the last few decades. There is plenty of anecdotal evidence to that point. One need not look further than the US Open in which a time of 4 hours was considered long in the days of Ben Hogan and Sam Snead while a round of 5 and a half hours is standard at today's championship.

At many public and daily fee courses, 5 hour rounds are common. In some cases, the rounds take six hours. I like to play golf for six hours, but I expect to play 36 holes in that time. How much of a problem is this? Is the extra hour (or two) significant? According to Frank Thomas' study and his follow up interviews, that extra hour amounts to something close to a tipping point. That extra hour can turn a half day commitment into what seems to be a full day's. It cannot be said with certainty, but it is not unreasonable to believe that that extra hour has discouraged a sizeable number of golfers from playing more golf.

Of course it could just be an excuse. There could be other reasons which people don't want to admit to which are the real culprits. Other reasons could be pressure at the office or home. But even in those cases, time must be a factor in making the decision to play or not.

Whether it is a real cause or an excuse, there is no reason not to try to get the pace back in line with an average of 4 hours or less on a typical course. Most people would say that this – *the time to play 18 holes* - is the real problem. Getting the typical round back to 4 hours would likely go a long way to bring back interest in the game.

## Waiting Time to Hit

But to others, waiting on every shot is more important than overall time to play. This problem - *the total waiting time until it is your turn to hit as a result of waiting for the group ahead to clear the landing zone over the course of an 18 hole round* - is under-represented at least by the general discussion in the media. (The time waiting to hit while waiting for other players in your own group is particularly excruciating, but that's the company you keep. Three/45 Golfers lead by example and provide positive instruction to get their own fellow competitors to pick up the pace.)

It is quite possible that "waiting on every shot" is far more of a problem for the enjoyment of the game than the overall time to play, and it may be a significant factor driving regular golfers from playing more. Although the overall time to play may be what's driving people away from the game, waiting to hit on every shot is a huge deterrent to the *enjoyment* of the game.

MIT Professor Richard Larson is probably the world's leading waiting time analysis expert. After building the most sophisticated mathematical models of waiting time for everything from waiting for your bags at the airport to waiting for the police to respond to a crime, he came to the conclusion that it is often not how long you, wait but how you wait. Unoccupied (just standing around) wait time is the most annoying. And waiting time for no good reason is particularly aggravating. That pretty much describes waiting for the group ahead to clear or waiting on a par 3 tee until the group (or groups) ahead finish. It might not add up to a lot of time, but it sure ruins the day.

My research indicates that it is not unlikely that two groups can play in the same amount of overall time, but one can have far more waiting time to hit shots. If the first group is "slow", they will not wait on shots but the group behind them will wait on almost every shot. Although both groups will likely play in about the same time the second will be far more frustrated and complain that the round was a miserable experience.

Is this a different problem than the first? Yes and actually may be exacerbated as we speed up play. As groups get faster, they may not get faster at the same rate, thus causing some golfers to wait on some shots, even though the overall pace has improved. Interestingly, the total waiting time for the group ahead to clear is in many cases unrelated to the total time to play 18 holes. Groups can play slowly but be spread far apart, thus not causing any shot delay, while at another time all the groups could be "fast" but are so close together any variation in playing time would result in shot delays.

This problem, the percentage or total amount of time on the course for which you are waiting for the group ahead to clear, is grossly under researched and not understood. I will discuss this later in the book.

## Revenue Management

As said above, to course owners, golf is a business. As much as they love the game, if they don't earn a profit, their course will soon become a real estate development. To private club managers, they want to please as many members as possible when they want to be pleased. And publicly-owned courses want both, more revenue and more satisfied tax-paying golfers.

Does slow play hurt their bottom line? Logically you would think it can't help. That has to be true at least in the long run. If slow play is forcing people from the game, fewer rounds will be played and in turn less revenue will be realized or fewer members will be happy.

But as is true in other parts of this problem, improving one thing might hurt another. Contrary to common thought, efforts to increase revenue may be a major contributor to overall slow play. My research and that of others such as Bill Yates, indicate that if you put too many golfers on the course, you may make more money in the short run, but you will guarantee long rounds and lots of waiting.

## Conclusion

All of these are problems. The first is well recognized now and there are efforts on going to try to address the issue. The second is not nearly as well recognized and it is not clear if anyone has a good understanding of how to address it other than what I will present later in the book. The third remains a serious problem particularly at public links courses where the pressure to put as many golfers on the course at any one time has political implications as well as management concerns.

In this book, I hope to lay out a *Plan* which will address all three of these problems with the hope of improving all three situations. If implemented, this plan can greatly increase golfers' enjoyment and help strengthen the game.

# 3 SUGGESTED WAYS TO SPEED UP PLAY

Everyone has an idea of how to speed up play. Some people believe if everyone walked faster, the pace would be better. Some believe carts speed up play, others believe they slow things down. Some believe "conceding" short putts would speed up play. Others say that everyone should go to their own ball and be ready to hit when it is their turn to play. Others say practice swings should be eliminated.

There have been hundreds of articles written about the pace of play problem providing specific instructions on how to improve the situation. There are too many to enumerate. This author wrote one of those articles humorously summarizing many of those ideas in a 1987 Golf Digest issue [3.] Perhaps the best discussion of what individual golfers should do to speed up play can be found in Peter Mateer's book, The Return of the Four Hour Round [4.]

13

Would any of these actually speed up play? And if so, by how much? Some may be good for some situations but useless for others. What factors determine slow play? What factors determine total and distributed waiting time? How can total rounds played in a day be maximized? How can we find the answers to these questions?

Before discussing what the research says, let me point out an important fact found in the field of Operations Management. Many decades ago, the traditional, conventional approach taken by American industrial/commercial managers was that when things went poorly, yell at the workers. Of course this didn't help much and American products suffered in the competition against foreign made goods. But as our understanding of business processes improved, it was discovered that, far more often than not, the real problem was the "system" in which the workers (mostly capable, well intentioned workers) had to function. The Japanese approach was to recognize this, improve the "system", and involve the workers in improving productivity. The rest, as they say, is history.

In the debate as to what should be done to speed up play, the overwhelming amount (I estimate 95%) of the discussion is about the behaviors of the players (the workers in this case.) This book takes the position (based on research and experience) that although there is a lot to be done to educate and train golfers to have a better pace of play attitude, they are only one part of the problem and in some cases not the problem at all. Just keep that in mind.

**Author's Note: The next three chapters discuss the concepts and research which lead to the Three/45 Golf Association's Pace of Play Improvement Plan. Parts of them can be pretty dry. If you are not familiar with the research, it is highly recommended you read these chapters. But if you believe you have a good understanding of the complexity of the problem, you may skip to Chapter 7 and get right to the Plan.**

# 4 FACTORY PHYSICS

Before explaining the techniques used to study the problem, a brief explanation of the science of "factory physics" [5] is appropriate since the approach of this work is to consider the golf course a factory producing rounds played by groups of golfers. The science provides a framework for analysis and brings with it some insights into problems and solutions for moving product (groups of golfers) through a factory (the golf course.) After that discussion, a review of previous studies is offered and then the analysis is explained.

To explain the concepts of factory physics, some definitions are needed. Definitions for "processes", "operations", "throughput time", "cycle time", "capacity", "throughput rate", "work-in-process", and "bottlenecks" are offered to assist in the discussion of our analysis. Each is important to people who run factories and each has a special meaning and

16

importance to the issue of pace of play and total rounds played.

All factories consist of **processes** which when provided with the right resources, produce finished products. Processes are made up of individual **operations** generally done in a series. Each operation adds something (adds value) to the product. In our golf analogy, each hole is an operation and each foursome is a work-in-process product which becomes a finished product when the group completes the 18th hole.

In factory physics, the time it takes one unit of product to go through the whole process, from start to finish, to go from raw input to finished product, is called **Throughput Time**. That would be equivalent to the time it takes one group to play their full round of golf.

Another time measure is the time between successive outputs, or completed products, of a factory. Stated another way, when one unit comes out of a factory, how long will it be until the next finished unit comes out? That is called **Cycle Time.** In the world of golf, that would be the time between successive groups finishing the 18th hole.

These two time indicators measure very different things. The distinction is important for the discussion later. The descriptions above apply these definitions to the whole process, all 18 holes, but they can also be applied to each operation (each hole) as well. The throughput time for a hole would be the time from when a group arrives at a tee until they complete the hole, including the time to play the hole plus the time waiting on the tee to get started. On the other hand, the cycle time for that hole would be found by standing at the green and starting a stopwatch as one group walks away from the green having finished the hole and stopping it when the next group walks away after finishing the hole.

Throughput time in a factory is comprised of three things: time in which the product is actually being worked on (operation or value-added time), waiting time (time from when a unit arrived at an operation until work began on it at that operation), and transportation time (time needed to move it to the next operation.) In golf, playing the hole (hitting and moving) is operation time, waiting until the group ahead has cleared the landing zone or green complex is waiting time, and the time walking to the next tee from the previous green is transportation time. For this analysis, walking between strokes is considered part of operation time since it is part of playing the hole.

In a well-designed factory, operation time is a large percentage of throughput time. Very little of the time is spent waiting or moving the product. For a golf course to be a well-designed factory, waiting time and time between holes should be minimized. The original rules of golf published by the Honourable Company of Edinburgh in 1744 said "ye shall tee your ball no further than one club length from the previous hole" – and they meant the *hole itself*. Golf architects should take note of that.

The amount of product that comes out of the factory per unit time (per hour or per day) is called the **Throughput Rate** or just **Throughput** (not to be confused with Throughput Time.) In golf, the number of groups who finish their rounds per hour or per day is the throughput. Throughput determines revenue.

**Work In Process (WIP)** is the sum of all product in the factory which is in production but not yet finished. In golf WIP is the number of golfers on the course at any one time. In the factory a certain amount of WIP is needed to keep the factory "humming" and to maximize Throughput Rate. However too much WIP clogs the factory and increases Throughput Time. Factory Physics has techniques to find the right amount of WIP to keep Throughput Rate high but Throughput Time low.

Those techniques calculate an optimal amount of WIP, or in golf, an optimal amount of groups on the course. Once reached, that optimal amount should be held constant, or at least not exceeded. Any increase over that amount will lead to longer Throughput Times. The optimal amount will keep revenue up yet not slow down play. In golf, once that amount has been reached, groups should only be allowed onto the course at the same rate as they come off. The tee time interval is the key to maintaining an optimal number of groups on the course.

The **Capacity** of a factory is the maximum amount of product it can finish per time period, per hour or per day. Whether the factory is making cars or Oreo cookies or tee shirts, there is a limit to how many it can produce per time unit. All production systems have a limit. How much is the limit? How do you calculate that limit? Good managers are always looking for ways to maximize their capacity, to get the most out of their factory.

**Capacity** differs from **Throughput** in that throughput is the actual amount produced while capacity is the most the factory can produce if everything is in order. Throughput can be less than or equal to capacity, but not more. If the orders for a product come in at a rate less than the factory can produce, throughput will be equal to the demand. If the demand is greater than capacity, throughput will equal capacity. A factory with a capacity of 100 units per hour may have a throughput less than 100 if machines break down or if the demand is less than 100 per hour. In golf, a course may be able to "produce" seven groups each hour, but if only six groups show up, the throughput would only be six even though its capacity was seven.

Capacity is a critical concept. Measuring it and understanding its implications is central to understanding how to maximize the rounds played in a day. The capacity of a factory is equal to the capacity of the lowest capacity operation. If a factory has several operations done in series, the one that can produce the least per hour is the one that determines how many units the *entire* factory can produce per hour. The lowest capacity operation is called the **bottleneck**. If a factory had five steps to produce a product, and the operations at four of those steps could produce 10 units per hour and the fifth could produce 8 units per hour, the factory's capacity would be 8 units per hour. Increasing the capacity of a non-bottleneck operation does nothing for increasing the capacity of the factory. Increasing one of the 10 units per hour operations to 11 units per hour will do nothing for the capacity of the factory. To increase the capacity of the factory, the capacity of the bottleneck has to be increased.

Capacity is important to a golf course because it determines how many groups can finish per hour (throughput rate) during daylight hours. For most of the day (once the course is full), capacity, not throughput time, determines how many groups can finish in an hour. As shall be shown later, only at the end of the day (as the sun goes down) does throughput time have an effect on the total number of rounds played.

Another important aspect of capacity is that it is ephemeral. An airplane which takes off with an empty seat cannot add another seat on the next plane to make up for the lost production. In golf when a group goes out with three golfers, the lost "productivity" cannot be made up by putting out a group of five later that day.

In a factory, bottlenecks are found in a number of ways. First as explained above, a bottleneck is the operation in a process which has the lowest capacity (lowest output per unit time.) Second, the bottleneck operation has the highest machine or worker utilization rate. It is always busy since it always has work to do. Third a bottleneck is the one operation with work-in-process inventory (things to work on) building up in front of it.

Of the three ways to identify a bottleneck, the last measure is the most obvious and easiest to use. On a golf course, 3 pars are usually the bottlenecks, the holes where groups queue up waiting to tee off. Interestingly, it takes less time to play a par 3 (throughput time) than a par 5, but the par three is the bottleneck. That condition will be discussed at length later in this paper. (Hint: we need to understand a hole's cycle time as well as its throughput time.)

In its simplest form, a factory that makes one product has one bottleneck. The bottleneck operation constrains the entire factory. In golf the bottleneck, like in the factory, may be one part of the course. However in golf the "product" itself may be the bottleneck in that one very slow group will slow everyone down. This other dimension adds a level of complexity not usually found in factory analysis. This complication will be analyzed later in the paper.

Of all the factors just defined, some are mathematically related and some are not. For example, *capacity and cycle time are directly related.* One is the inverse of the other. If the factory can produce 8 units per hour, on average the time between successive finished units will be 7.5 minutes, sixty minutes divided by 8. If you know one, you know the other. If you increase capacity, you reduce cycle time, and vice versa.

On the other hand, *capacity and throughput time are only remotely related,* related only by the time it takes to get through the

LUCIUS RICCIO

bottleneck. For example in the five-operation factory discussed above, the capacity of the factory is equal to the capacity of the bottleneck, 8 units per hour. The other four operations have a capacity of 10 units per hour. The throughput time of this process is the sum of the times to complete all five operations. The time to get through the bottleneck operation (assuming no waiting time) would be 7.5 minutes, found by dividing 60 by 8 per hour. The time to get through each of the other four is 6 minutes found by dividing 60 by 10 per hour. Thus the total throughput time is 31.5 minutes.

If we now improved the capacity of one of the non-bottleneck operations to 12 per hour, the time to finish that operation would now be 5 minutes and overall throughput time would be improved. However, the factory can still only produce 8 per hour or one every 7.5 minutes, since the bottleneck has not changed. In that case, throughput time is improved but cycle time (and by definition throughput rate) is not changed. One lesson from this is changes may lead to the improvement in one measure of system performance but not others. In some cases it may lead to an improvement in one and a reduction in another. Understanding how all aspects work together, not just one or two, is critical to improving system performance.

One last point is important to this study. If the input rate to the system (factory unit orders per hour) is greater than the capacity of the bottleneck, work-in-process inventory will naturally build at the bottleneck. To insure WIP inventory doesn't build up at the bottleneck, the capacity of the bottleneck has to match or slightly exceed input rate. In the example above, if factory orders were coming in faster than 8 per hour, WIP inventory would build in front of the bottleneck since it can handle only 8 per hour.

Regarding this last point, golf courses tend to send out golfers from the first tee as soon as the group ahead clears the first hole's hitting zone. That time is often shorter than the cycle time of the bottleneck hole (typically a par three) thus resulting in a backup there. This problem will be discussed at length later.

# 5 PREVIOUS RESEARCH STUDIES

Although pace of play has long been a topic of discussion in the world of golf, surprisingly few serious studies of it have been undertaken. However two significant and well-done academic studies and at least one organizational analysis have been done.

Kimes and Schruben [6] studied golf course administration from a revenue management perspective. By simulating pace of play on a specific (unnamed) course using a discrete-event simulation model, they examined the relationship between tee time intervals and the time to play a round as well as the total number of groups a course could accommodate in a day. They found (as would be predicted by Factory Physics) that longer intervals between groups leads to shorter throughput times and that shortening tee time intervals is good up to a point after which there is a rapid deterioration in pace of play.

That point, of course, is when the tee time interval approaches the value predicted by the capacity of the bottleneck hole.

Tiger and Salzer [7] developed a simulation model of the daily play at a golf course primarily to use as a classroom simulation teaching aid. However their model was substantial enough to consider pace of play and course throughput concerns seriously. They concluded that the bottlenecks on many courses are the 3 pars and that a "wave up" strategy could improve throughput by over 10%.

While both studies were well done, several issues that could affect the pace of play and course throughput were not studied. In particular how does player variability affect pace of play? Does walking faster reduce throughput time more than clearing the green faster? Is there a trade-off of total time to play and individual shot waiting time? A model with more robust capabilities was needed.

A substantial amount of work has been done by Yates [8] using an approach developed by Dean Knuth, former Director of Handicapping for the USGA, called the USGA Pace Rating System [9.] The system evaluates golf courses to rate the pace at which golfers should play a course given its difficulty and other factors. This system provides guidelines for how long it should take to play a course with the notion that each course has a pace "blueprint" (my word.) Yates advises courses on how to improve their pace of play, all along recognizing the limitations imposed by the physical nature of the course.

In summary, Kimes focused on the slow play issue from a tee time interval management perspective (how does management's tee interval decision affect pace?), Tiger from a player characteristic standpoint (how do player behaviors affect pace?) and Yates from a course design point of view (how does the course affect pace?) The Three/45 Pace of Play Principles ® and The Plan for Improvement ® attempts to bring all of this together and consider all perspectives.

It should also be noted that the people mention above are real heroes (given the title of this book maybe saints is a better term) in the battle for a quicker pace of play. They have done ground breaking work and generally get no recognition for the hard work and good results they have achieved. My hat is off to them and others like them.

# 6 MODELS OF PACE OF PLAY

In order to examine this issue in more depth and develop a science of pace of play, several models were developed to consider different aspects of the problem. First a simulation of one group playing one whole (*Single Group/Single Hole*) was built to assist in the study of how one group's behavior can affect their pace of play. Another model was a spreadsheet analysis (*Single Hole Bottleneck Analysis*) to explain how, in general, certain holes become either bottlenecks or non-bottleneck holes. A third was developed to study overall playing time and waiting time for many groups playing on an 18 hole course (*18 holes/Multiple Groups.*) This model was used two ways. First it was run assuming constant times to play shots and to move from shot to shot (*Deterministic.*) Second it was set up to include several more realistic and varied assumptions (*Multiple Groups With Variability*), specifically the natural variability in taking shots and moving to the next one. Fourth a series of queueing models were built to give greater insight into why there is waiting at some par 4s and not others. Lastly a model using Kimes' [6] results was built to examine the pace of play consequences of course management's understandable desire to maximize revenue. All of these proved helpful in uncovering an understanding of the problem from different perspectives.

## Single Group/Single Hole Model

The single group/single hole model simulated the individual strokes and movement of each player in a group of four to complete the play of a hole.

Each player in the group had a shot pattern distribution for each type of stroke. Several player movement disciplines were tested. They ranged from "all moving to the nearest ball and waiting for that player to hit before moving to their own balls" or "all moving to their own ball first." Two versions were tested: one with fixed times and one with variable times.

Three movement-disciplines were tested for a version with fixed times. The first had all golfers move to the position of the shortest tee ball with all waiting until the first hits his second shot, then everyone advancing to the next shortest, waiting until that player hits, etc. until all have hit. The second discipline had everyone move to their own ball, but waiting until the previous player hits until they begin the pre-shot planning. The third discipline has everyone move to their own ball and immediately begin their pre-shot planning.

In its simplest form, the model can be explained as follows. In the first discipline, it is assumed that each player has a 30 second pre-shot routine and a 15 second ball striking routine, and that it takes each player an additional 15 seconds to walk to the next closest ball. In the first discipline, it takes 3 minutes and 45 seconds for the group to clear the landing area. In the second discipline, it takes the group 3 minutes to clear the area. In the third it takes only 1 and one half minutes. These results indicate that golfers' individual movement/preparation strategies can make a significant difference in the time it takes to clear a landing area. Assuming the savings could be realized, the difference between the first and third disciplines can save as much as one hour per round.

A second model used the same spreadsheets but used variable times instead of fixed times. This model demonstrated clearly that the pace of the group is almost exclusively the pace of the slow player if there is one dominant slow player. If the players are basically similar, the time to play the hole is determined by the sum of the slowest played strokes at each stage of the hole.

Single Group/ Single Shot

Time To Play Hole (Seconds)

| Player | 0 | 45 | 60 | 75 | 90 | 105 | 120 | 135 | 150 | 165 | 180 | 195 | 210 | 225 |
|---|---|---|---|---|---|---|---|---|---|---|---|---|---|---|
| | | | | | | | | | | | | | | |

Everyone Waits At First Player Before Moving

| 1 | Play | Walk | Wait | Wait | Wait | Walk | Wait | Wait | Wait | Walk | Wait | Wait | Wait | Wait |
| 2 | Wait | Walk | Play | Play | Play | Walk | Wait | Wait | Wait | Walk | Wait | Wait | Wait | Wait |
| 3 | Wait | Walk | Wait | Wait | Wait | Walk | Play | Play | Play | Walk | Wait | Wait | Wait | Wait |
| 4 | Wait | Walk | Wait | Wait | Wait | Walk | Wait | Wait | Wait | Walk | Play | Play | Play | Play |

Walk But Wait Before Pre-Shot Routine Starts

| 1 | Play | Walk | Wait | Wait | Walk | Wait | Wait | Walk | Wait | Wait | | | | |
| 2 | Walk | Play | Play | Play | Walk | Wait | Wait | Walk | Wait | Wait | | | | |
| 3 | Walk | Wait | Wait | Wait | Play | Play | Play | Walk | Wait | Wait | | | | |
| 4 | Walk | Walk | Wait | Wait | Walk | Wait | Wait | Play | Play | Play | | | | |

Walk to Own Ball and Hit When Your Turn

| 1 | Play | Walk | Walk | Walk |
| 2 | Walk/Pre | Play | Walk | Walk |
| 3 | Walk | Pre Shot | Play | Walk |
| 4 | Walk | Wait/Pre | Pre Shot | Play |

## Single Hole Bottleneck Analysis Model

The bottleneck analysis model is a spreadsheet model which assumed fixed times for a group to tee off, to walk to the next hitting area, time to clear that hitting area, and lastly the time to clear the green and allow the next group to hit up. The model simulated the play of several groups first through a par 3, then a par 4, and then a par 5, and lastly a par 3 in which the following group was "waved up" (allowed to play while the previous group waited before putting out.) The analysis assumed all groups tee off in 3 minutes, take three minutes to walk to the next stroke (to the green on par 3s), 3 minutes to clear the second on par 4s and 5s and, on par 5s, the third shot. It assumed it took two minutes to walk to the green on par 4s, and two minutes on par 5s after the second shot to walk to the third, and two minutes after the third shot to the green. It assumed all groups on all holes took 4 minutes to clear the green.

Using these figures, it would take a group 10 minutes to play a par 3 (3 minutes to tee off, 3 minutes to walk to the green and 4 minutes to clear the green.) It would take a group 15 minutes to finish a par 4 (3 + 3 + 3 + 2 + 4) and 20 minutes to play a par 5 (3 + 3 + 3 + 2 + 3 + 2 + 4.) Those times would be the throughput times for each of those holes. An uninformed observer might conclude that since the par 5 takes the longest, it must be the bottleneck. However our experience tells us that par 3s tend to be bottleneck holes, even though they take the shortest time to play.

The reason our experience is correct is because the bottleneck is not determined by throughput time, but by capacity. Looking at the par 3, the first group plays the hole in 10 minutes. At that point the next group can start and it plays the hole in 10 minutes. Each subsequent group plays it in ten minutes. The time between successive groups is 10 minutes. That is the definition of cycle time. (In this case, throughput time equals cycle time since this is just one hole and we have not added any waiting time.)

As explained before, capacity is directly (inversely) related to cycle time. As such the capacity of the par 3 is 60 minutes divided by 10, or 6 groups per hour.

The par 4 throughput time is 14 minutes for the first group to play. However the next group cannot begin play until after the first group hits its second shots and clears the hitting area. In the paper by Tiger et al, this is called clearing the "gate." We have adopted a similar concept in our simulations.

The second group cannot hit their second shots until the first group clears the green. The spreadsheet models shows that using these time estimates, the second group and each subsequent group must wait one minute for the group ahead to clear the green before they can begin hitting their second shots. As such the second group and each group after it will take 15 minutes to play the hole (throughput time.) However the model indicates that the time between groups starting and finishing the hole is 9 minutes (cycle time.) A cycle time of 9 minutes means the capacity of the hole is 6 and two thirds groups per hour. Interestingly, the throughput time (the time to play the hole) is larger than the throughput time for the par three but the cycle time is lower leading to a higher capacity for the par four than that of the par 3.

A similar analysis for par 5s shows that their capacity is the same as the par 4s. Given that the capacity of the par 3s is lower than the capacity of the others, they are by definition the bottlenecks. But just having the lowest capacity is not the only cause of delays at them. Most courses start with a par 4 or 5. Groups generally start as soon as the previous group clears the hitting zone (the first "gate.") Tee sheets usually set tee time intervals close to this time. Owners want to accommodate as many groups as possible and players get anxious to start. They want to get going as soon as they can. As shown above, the capacity of par 4s and 5s is 6 and 2/3rds per hour or one group every 9 minutes. As such new groups enter the course every 9 minutes. Courses with pace of play problems typically have tee intervals shorter than the bottleneck, usually less than nine minutes.

Since the capacity of a par 3 is 6 per hour, if groups arrive there at the rate of 6 and 2/3rds per hour, a queue has to build up. This simple model demonstrates why our experience makes sense. **The optimal tee time interval for pace of play is equal to the cycle time of the hole with the lowest capacity (highest cycle time,) generally the par 3s, not the opening hole.** Sending groups out at a rate faster than the capacity of the bottleneck creates delays and significantly slows the overall pace of play.

As mentioned the model also tested the effect of "waving up" on a par 3. In that situation, the first group stops playing once they reach the green and waits for the next group to hit (3 minutes in this model) their tee shots. After the following group finishes teeing off, they putt out (clear the green.) Using this approach for all groups, the time to play the hole (throughput time) goes up. For the first group, the time to play the hole goes up to 13 minutes and for each subsequent group it goes up to 14 minutes since it takes each group 3 minutes to reach the green, but the previous group takes 4 minutes to clear the green. As such an additional minute is added to the throughput time.

However because of "waving up", each new group can tee off 7 minutes after the previous group teed off. As such the cycle time drops to 7 minutes and the capacity of the hole goes up to 8 and 4/7ths. Note: the throughput time went up but the cycle time went down.

An increase in capacity at the bottleneck would allow the course to accommodate more groups per hour. Note that by doing this, the capacity of the course is now not constrained by the par 3s. The capacity of the par 4s and par 5s remains at 6 and 2/3rds and as such they become the new bottlenecks. Some improvement has been realized but not the full amount unless something is done to improve the capacity of the par 4 and 5 holes as well.

This model can help pinpoint how the different parts of playing a hole can affect the time to play the hole and the capacity of the hole. For example, using the numbers above for a par 4 as a base case, the model will indicate what happens to those measures if the players walk faster or slower, take more or less time to tee off or play their second shots or clear the green.

The base case for the par 4 assumed 3 minutes to tee off, 2 minutes to walk to the second shot area (the first "gate"), 3 minutes to play toward the green, 2 minutes to walk to the green complex, and 4 minutes to clear the green. If all players in all groups either teed off or walked slower by one minute, there would be no change to either the throughput time or cycle time. The extra minute at the front end of the hole does not result in any improvement because the base case has a one minute wait at the second shot while the lead group clears the green. This confirms the experience of many regular golfers who realize it is not "worth" speeding up play at the front of a hole. It is, as they say in the army, "hurry up and wait." As a result, many golfers just don't hurry up, leading to bad habits that carry over to other parts of play.

On the other hand, speeding up or slowing down at the back

end of the hole has significant effects. Speeding up (or slowing down) by one minute either in the walk to the green or clearing the green reduces (or adds) 2 minutes to the throughput time and one minute to the cycle time. One of the two minutes saved on throughput time is the one minute of faster play and the other is the one minute of waiting time in the fairway.

The lesson here is that a minute saved can, in one place, improve nothing and, in another place, be worth more than a minute. It is important to understand what parts of play have a significant effect on pace of play and capacity.

One of the rules of factory physics is to design the process with the bottleneck near the beginning of the process. In this case the bottleneck for the hole is clearing the green. Any delay at the green causes backups all the way back to the tee. For a par 4 to work well, the hole should be designed to allow the players to clear the green faster than it takes to tee off and walk to their balls. It is hard and somewhat foolish to slow players at any part of play even the front end, so speeding up clearing the green is the smart strategy. Of course some architects have "solved" (not improved) this problem by including long walks from green to tee, which has the effect of slowing down the teeing portion of the hole. On the other hand by waving up on a par 3, the time the group takes until it tees off on the next hole is, in essence, increased.

## Par 3

### No Wave Up

| | Time | Group Number | | | | | | | |
|---|---|---|---|---|---|---|---|---|---|
| | | 1 | 2 | 3 | 4 | 5 | 6 | 7 | 8 |
| Tee | 3 | 3 | 13 | 23 | 33 | 43 | 53 | 63 | 73 |
| Walk | 3 | 6 | 16 | 26 | 36 | 46 | 56 | 66 | 76 |
| Green | 4 | 10 | 20 | 30 | 40 | 50 | 60 | 70 | 80 |
| *Thru-Put Time* | | *10* | *10* | *10* | *10* | *10* | *10* | *10* | *10* |

### With Wave Up

| | | 1 | 2 | 3 | 4 | 5 | 6 | 7 | 8 |
|---|---|---|---|---|---|---|---|---|---|
| Tee | 3 | 3 | 9 | 16 | 23 | 30 | 37 | 44 | 51 |
| Walk | 3 | 6 | 12 | 19 | 26 | 33 | 40 | 47 | 54 |
| Wait | | 9 | 16 | 23 | 30 | 37 | 44 | 51 | 58 |
| Green | 4 | 13 | 20 | 27 | 34 | 41 | 48 | 55 | 62 |
| *Thru-Put Time* | | *13* | *14* | *14* | *14* | *14* | *14* | *14* | *14* |
| *Cycle Time* | | | *7* | *7* | *7* | *7* | *7* | *7* | *7* |

## Par 4 Hole

| | | 1 | 2 | 3 | 4 | 5 | 6 | 7 | 8 |
|---|---|---|---|---|---|---|---|---|---|
| Tee | 3 | 3 | 12 | 21 | 30 | 39 | 48 | 57 | 66 |
| Walk | 3 | 6 | 15 | 24 | 33 | 42 | 51 | 60 | 69 |
| Fairway Shot | 3 | 9 | 18 | 27 | 36 | 45 | 54 | 63 | 72 |
| Walk | 2 | 11 | 20 | 29 | 38 | 47 | 56 | 65 | 74 |
| Green | 4 | 15 | 24 | 33 | 42 | 51 | 60 | 69 | 78 |
| *Thru-Put Time* | | *15* | *15* | *15* | *15* | *15* | *15* | *15* | *15* |
| *Cycle Time* | | | *9* | *9* | *9* | *9* | *9* | *9* | *9* |

## Par 5 Hole

| | | 1 | 2 | 3 | 4 | 5 | 6 | 7 | 8 |
|---|---|---|---|---|---|---|---|---|---|
| Tee | 3 | 3 | 12 | 21 | 30 | 39 | 48 | 57 | 66 |
| Walk | 3 | 6 | 15 | 24 | 33 | 42 | 51 | 60 | 69 |
| Fairway Shot | 3 | 9 | 18 | 27 | 36 | 45 | 54 | 63 | 72 |
| Walk | 2 | 11 | 20 | 29 | 38 | 47 | 56 | 65 | 74 |
| Fairway Shot | 3 | 14 | 23 | 32 | 41 | 50 | 59 | 68 | 77 |
| Walk | 2 | 16 | 25 | 34 | 43 | 52 | 61 | 70 | 79 |
| Green | 4 | 20 | 29 | 38 | 47 | 56 | 65 | 74 | 83 |
| *Thru-Put Time* | | *20* | *20* | *20* | *20* | *20* | *20* | *20* | *20* |
| *Cycle Time* | | | *9* | *9* | *9* | *9* | *9* | *9* | *9* |

Another application of the concept of having the bottleneck

early on in a process is to have the bottleneck hole be the first hole. If courses were designed with the longest par 3 as the first hole and there was no waving up, the rest of the course would flow smoothly. You would never put more groups on the course than the course can adequately accommodate from a pace of play perspective. But as we shall see later, this might not please course management in their desire to maximize revenue.

## 18 Hole/Multiple Group Simulation

## With Deterministic Times

To obtain far more detailed answers to the more significant questions raised, a full course simulation model with many groups playing in natural succession (almost a full day of play) was built similar but with more details to the models of Kimes and Tiger.

This simulation modeled each group's progression through the course shot by shot using a "gate" approach similar to that used by Tiger. The time it took a group to tee off, to move to the next shot, to complete that next shot, etc. until reaching the green and then the time to clear the green was modeled. The following group would tee off on hole 1 at the prescribed tee time interval or at the time the preceding group cleared the fairway whichever was later, and then proceeded at their own pace until they were "held up" by the preceding group's progress. In the model, they waited to begin their next shots until the preceding group cleared the next "gate" or the green.

In this first version, the model assumed that all shot sequences for a group were deterministic, constant. For a particular group their group's total time to tee off or play a fairway shot was a constant for all holes they played, the speed to move to their next shot was a constant speed, and their time to clear the green was a constant for all holes.

Thirty groups were sent off on a typical 6600 yard course. The model was set up to test any combination of shot and movement paces. Each group could be characterized as "Fast" or "Slow." For discussion the following metrics were used to demonstrate the generalized findings.

The Fast groups clear the tee and fairway shots in 3 minutes (45 seconds per shot), the green in 3 minutes and move at 3 MPH (90 yards per minute.) Those parameters would allow each group, *if unimpeded,* to play 18 holes in 241 minutes, just about 4 hours. Several versions of the Slow groups were considered. The typical test was to have them clear shots in 4 minutes, the green in 4 minutes and walk at 2 MPH (60 yards per minute.) The model was run with all Fast groups, then all

Slow groups and, finally, with combinations of both.

From the Single Hole/Single Group model, we found that individual shot management and logistics can add a substantial amount of time to the play of a particular shot and, subsequently, to the time to play a hole. From the Bottleneck model we found that the capacity of the course can be determined by the hole that takes the shortest time to play, the par 3s, rather than the longest hole and that par 3 capacity can be affected by the wave up policy.

The Deterministic 18 Hole Model was used to test Tee Time Intervals, to test various combinations of the speed groups play their shots and move, and to test various combinations of fast play and slow play golfers on the course at the same time.

## All Groups Playing at the Same Pace:

*Tee Interval Comparison*

Even though we know that not all groups play at the same pace, it is worth examining further the dynamics of pace for this situation. If each group played at those rates and was sent out in 9 minute intervals, every group would play in 241 minutes and there would be essentially no waiting time. With no waving up, the par 3s set the capacity of the course. The time to play each of the par threes ranged from 8.2 minutes to 8.7. As such a tee time interval of 9 was appropriate. The model was tested with other tee times with the following results:

Table 1

| Tee Time Interval | Average Time to Play | Maximum Time to Play |
|:---:|:---:|:---:|
| 9 | 241 | 241 |
| 8 | 250 | 260 |
| 7 | 265 | 290 |

The maximum times are for the last group of the day. With an interval lower than the cycle time of the bottleneck hole, groups will bunch and wait. The time to play steadily increases over the course of the day. The first group still plays in 241 minutes but each successive group takes longer, getting close to 5 hours to play. Here is the graph of the results for all fast players but with an 8 minute tee interval:

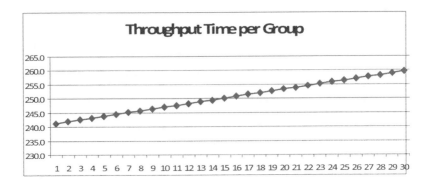

*Walking Speed Comparison*

In this model, tee time intervals greater than 9 minutes do nothing for pace of play if the speed is at least 3mph. But at 2mph, a greater interval is needed to keep the pace at 4 hours. Even a 10 minute interval is not enough, causing the pace to jump to 277 minutes, almost 40 minutes more.

What if all groups walked more slowly? Well, obviously the overall pace would slow. What if they played their shots slower? How much would that slow down play? Are there some shots more important than others? Is walking pace more important than shot time? This model can help with those questions.

With a 9 minute interval, by varying the walking speed, we get the following statistics (90 yards per minute equates to about 3mph and 60 to 2mph):

Table 2

| Speed (Yards/Minute) | Average Time | Maximum Time |
|:---:|:---:|:---:|
| 90 | 241 | 241 |
| 80 | 251 | 251 |
| 70 | 267 | 272 |
| 60 | 290 | 302 |

Here is the graph for the run with all groups moving at 2 mph (60 yards/minute):

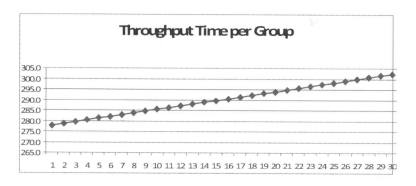

Note that the first group which is unimpeded by anyone plays at close to a 4 and one half hour rate.

From this it is clear that for a course and tee time interval capable of supporting a four hour round for everyone, when groups play their shots fast but walk slowly, the time to play will progressively increase over the course of the day from 4 hours to over 5 hours, this just because of slow movement.

Is slow play movement worse than slow play hitting? From these runs, walking at 2mph rather than 3mph will raise the average time to play by about 50 minutes and the maximum time by 60 minutes. How does that compare to slow hitting? With a 9 minute interval and groups moving at 3mph but taking an extra minute to clear each tee and fairway shot and an extra minute to clear the green, the average time jumps to 319 and the maximum to 342! As such slow hitting on every shot is far worse than just moving slowly.

## Combinations of Fast and Slow Groups

Although the results so far are illuminating, a better use of the model is to see what happens when slow players are thrown into the mix with fast players. In a field of all fast players, the model was run with the 5th group as a slow group (one slow group among fast groups.) The fast group cleared the tee, fairway and green in 3 minutes and moved at 3mph (90 yards/minute.)

The slow group played shots slower, cleared the green slower and/or moved slower. Various combinations of those were tested.

*Walking Speed Variation*

First, movement-pace was tested. Assuming the slow groups played their shots and cleared the green as fast as the fast players but moved slower, the model found the following results:

Table 3

| SlowGroup Speed(Yards/Minute) | AverageTime | MaxTime | Group MaxWait |
|---|---|---|---|
| 80 | 245 | 251 | 9 |
| 70 | 255 | 262 | 20 |
| 60 | 268 | 278 | 35 |

Recall that the first 4 groups, unimpeded by the slow group, played in 241 minutes. The max time is the time the slow group played. As can be seen by the graph below, the 6th group could play just slightly faster than the slow group, and each successive group played just a small amount faster but nowhere near the time they could play in if unimpeded. The average time takes all groups into account and Max wait is the total wait time the 6th group has to suffer. This is with only one slow group. As more slow groups are added the figures get worse.

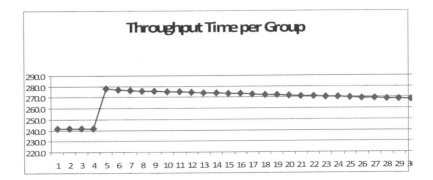

At 60 Yards/minute (2mph) even groups who don't dawdle over their shots add more than a half hour to their round by moving more slowly. But the real tragedy is that every group after them suffers, boosting the day's average play close to 30 minutes more than it has to be. You cannot play faster than the group ahead. If you are behind a slow group, speeding up does no good. This leads to bad habits. It is easier to learn bad habits than good habits.

The following is the plot of the total time each group waits in this scenario:

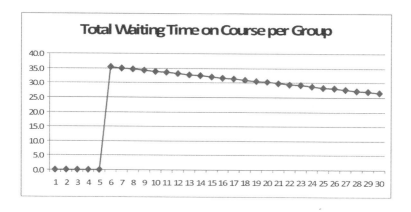

The first four groups play fast and have no waiting time. The 5th group is the slow one and they don't wait as well. But the 6th group is stuck. They could play in four hours if unimpeded. But they can't play faster than the group ahead. Each group after that play just slightly faster since they can play the first few holes quickly until they catch up to the queue.

*Walking Speed Variation with Tight Tee Interval*

With an 8 minute tee interval, the numbers get worse:

Table 4

|  | Average | Maximum | Wait |
|---|---|---|---|
| 60 Yards/Min | 281 | 300 | 54 |

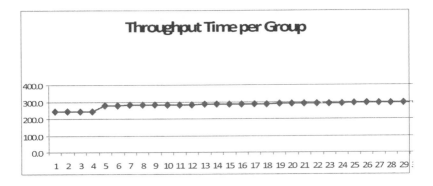

The slow group now plays in 5 hours, everyone averages 4 hours and 40 minutes and the poor 6th group waits a total of close to one hour. That is one extra hour of standing around. That is far more tiring. As my friend Arthur Little says "museums are tiring because of all the standing." What this means is with a tee interval below the bottleneck pace, one slow group sets the pace for everyone that follows. *There is little the following groups can do to improve things, which leads to great frustration.*

*Stroke Preparation and Hitting Pace*

With a 9 minute interval, what would happen if the slow group moved at 3mph but hit their shots more slowly, clearing the tee, fairway or green in 4 rather than 3 minutes? In this model it turns out that it doesn't matter if we add the minute to any one of the three shot types. The results are the same:

Table 5

| | Average | Maximum | Wait |
|---|---|---|---|
| 9 Minute Interval<br><br>4 Minute Clearing with 3mph | 252 | 259 | 18 |

:

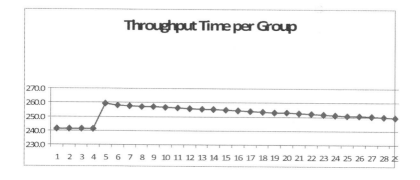

*Tee Interval with Slow Hitting and Clearing*

The above result is understandable. We've added one minute

to each hole. The extra time doesn't add much bunching. But with an 8 minute interval, more bunching and longer times occur:

Table 6

| | Average | Maximum | Wait |
|---|---|---|---|
| 8 Minute Interval<br><br>4 Minute Clearing with 3mph | 266 | 278 | 21 |

Note the difference in the graph above and the one below. Below each successive group is playing more slowly. That is just due to the tee interval.

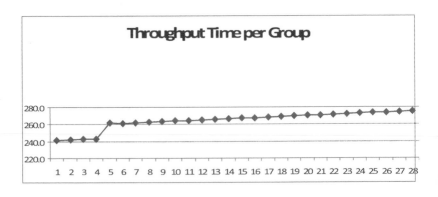

Back to a 9 minute interval, what would happen if the slow

group moved at 3mph but took 5 minutes to clear one of their shot-types, say clear the green. Here are the results:

Table 7

|  | Average | Maximum | Wait |
|---|---|---|---|
| 9 Minute Interval  5 Minute Clearing with 3mph | 267 | 279 | 35 |

Understandably the extra minute added another 18 (or so due to rounding for this study) minutes to the round compared to the 4 minute clearing run. But a better comparison is to the run with 9 minute interval, 3 minute clearing and only 2mph.The results are essentially identical. That means that walking slowly (2mphrather than 3mph) produces the same results as dawdling on the green for two extra minutes.

*Slow Hitting and Clearing*

What if the group was fast moving but slow hitting *all* shots? If they took 4 minutes to clear each shot but moved at 3mph, the results are as follows:                                    :

Table 8

|  | Average | Maximum | Wait |
|---|---|---|---|
| 9 Minute Interval<br><br>4 Minute Clearing All 3mph | 283 | 295 | 52 |

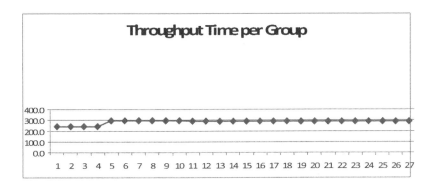

Again this is explainable in simple terms. This adds 2 minutes per hole more than the   case of hitting only one shot slowly. But the results are pretty strong. This leads to a round of almost 5 hours for almost everyone even though everyone moved fast. The PGA Tour faces this problem. Their players move to their balls quickly but then are very deliberate in making their strokes.

One last run was made with this model. How bad would it be

if the slow group took 4 minutes for clearing every shot and moved at 2mph? The results are, as expected, pretty grim:

Table 9

|  | Average | Maximum | Wait |
|---|---|---|---|
| 9 Minute Interval<br><br>4 Minute Clearing All 2mph | 314 | 340 | 90 |

The slow group played in 5 hours 40 minutes, the average play was over 5 hours and the 6th group had to suffer by waiting a total of 90 minutes. I was too afraid to try this combo with an 8 minute interval - an interval many if not most public courses use!

What if there was more than one slow group? If a second slow group was sent out in, say, the 10th game, the pace would revert back to the slow group's pace. Again everyone behind that group could go no faster than the slow group no matter how well they implemented fast play principles.

The results for these combination runs were enlightening. The most significant finding of course was that **the pace of play for everyone on a course is set by the slow group ahead of them.** The closer a group is to the slow group the greater effect, but there is always some effect until the slow group finishes.

One last note on this topic was an interesting finding by Tiger [7] he uncovered when studying the pace of pros and amateurs. He found that pros play tee-to-green much faster than amateurs but amateurs tend to clear the green faster. (We've all seen the pros take an un-godly amount of time on putts.) This is a lethal combination. It explains why pro-am events often take 5 to 6 hours to play.

## Bottleneck Analysis Model with Variable (Stochastic) Times

The previous discussion was based on a model in which each group's time to play the various parts of the game was fixed. That is, it took them exactly, say, 3 minutes to tee off on each hole. Or it took them exactly 4 minutes to clear each green. That model was helpful in understanding the essentials of bottleneck analysis and the concepts of throughput time and cycle time. The only variability introduced was that some (slow) groups took longer to play each shot or walked slower than other (fast) groups. The effect was substantial. If everyone played at the same pace and were sent off at the proper tee interval (higher for slower players), there would be no waiting. Waiting occurred when there was a difference.

In this new model, variability in the play of *each and every shot* is introduced. No one takes *exactly* the same amount of time each time to do anything. We all experience variability. In golf we all have lost a ball, hit a provisional, or had fiercely breaking putts that resulted in 3 slow attempts to finish out. These and many other situations lead to variation in the time it takes us to play various shots and the time to finish a hole.

Although variety may be the spice of life, in factory physics, variability is the enemy. Any form of variability leads to more cost, less production, quality issues and time delays. In golf, variability can only lead to slower play. Instinct might say that the variability would average out, but it doesn't.

One group playing slower and another faster does not result in a cancellation of slow play. Consider two groups of similar playing-time ability playing two consecutive holes. If the first group plays the first hole slowly then the next one fast and the following group plays the second slowly, the second group (because it had to wait for the first group to clear the first hole) "plays" both holes slowly. The variability doesn't cancel, it adds, it accumulates.

This version of the model includes the variability of playing time for all shots. It starts with groups of similar time-playing potential, but adds fluctuations when a shot is taken. It is assumed that variability on the slow side is more than on the fast side. *There is an absolute limit as to how fast you can play but almost no limit to how slowly you can play.* If you generally take 45 seconds to hit your tee ball, speeding up may lower that to 30 seconds, but if you have to hit a provisional it jumps to 90 seconds. As such it is assumed there is more variability potential on the up side.

Running this model with all groups of similar time-playing ability found that as you add more variability, average throughput times increased and overall waiting time increased. That was expected. What was interesting is that even when the groups were "equal", there was still a substantial amount of waiting time and that that waiting time was widely divergent. As suggested by the discussion above, waiting time accumulates when even "fast" groups played some holes slowly. As each group played one hole slowly, the wait time accumulated.

The following results are for runs with all "fast" groups but with some variability to the shot times, green clearing times, and moving paces. All runs use a 9 minute tee interval. The first run assumed a low level of variability (nearly deterministic times), the second a moderate amount of variability, and the third a substantial amount. The *average* shot times, green clearing times and walking paces were the same in all cases. The only thing that changes from run to run was the *variability*. Since there is a limit to how fast one can play but almost no limit to how slowly you can play, the variability was assumed to be somewhat more on the high side. Various distributions were tried. The displayed results were for runs using a triangle distribution, as Tiger had used.

Table 10

|  | Average Time | Maximum Time |
|---|---|---|
| Little Variability | 242 | 244 |
| Modest Variability | 278 | 294 |
| Significant Variability | 324 | 362 |

These are all "fast" groups in that their average times to play and move would allow them to play in 4 hours. As variability is added, averages go out the window and the total time to play goes up substantially. How can this be?

First the upside bias of the time to play shots and to move

raises the average somewhat. Second in a system of random events, the "negatives" are not always balanced by the "positives." If the group ahead plays a hole slowly, you have to wait and likely the group behind you has to wait. If later *you* play a hole slowly, the group behind you has to wait again. Their waiting time is the sum of the two times. If the group ahead and your group continue to play at a normal pace, the "lost" time is not made up. It just accumulates.

It is hard to make up time. A group that takes 5 more minutes to play a hole due to a lost ball, likely cannot play the next hole 5 minutes faster. **As such the pace is not set by the slowest group, but by the slowest play on each hole by all groups. It is not the average play but the sum of the slowest play on each hole.**

Using all golfers having "4 hour round" average pace of play characteristics except a high variance hitting tee and fairway shots only produces an average time to play of 294 minutes. The sum of the maximum time to play each hole by all the groups was 290. These similarities were found in other runs with different combinations of variability. It is not a perfect relationship, but it is in general true that the delays accumulate.

Earlier it was pointed out that the pace for all golfers was set by the slowest group. This model indicates that the pace is set by all groups by adding the slowest play for one or a few holes of each group and not their average or better play. **The pace is closer to the sum of each group's worst play. Everyone is now involved. Everyone is part of the problem.** Put another way, a group can be a "fast" group for most of the round yet still contribute to the overall slow pace by playing one or two holes slowly.

Of course Tee Intervals pose an additional problem. Shortening the internal when there is significant variability makes for very long rounds. Here are some results assuming significant variability:

Table 11

| Tee Interval | Average Time | Maximum Time |
|:---:|:---:|:---:|
| 12 | 298 | 324 |
| 10 | 310 | 348 |
| 9 | 324 | 362 |
| 8 | 338 | 377 |

Variability in shot times and movement pace combined with short intervals is a recipe for disaster. The model was re-run with moderate variability and even then a 10 minute interval created a four and a half hour round. **Clearly it is not just the golfers. Course management is part of the problem as well.**

Back to the golfers, are there some combinations of shot time variability, green clearing variability and movement pace variability better or worse than others? Combinations were tested all using the same average values but adding some variability as indicated. Here are the results:

Table 12

| Variability Level | | | Average Time | Maximum Time |
|---|---|---|---|---|
| Shots | Green | Movement | | |
| Low | High | Low | 262 | 274 |
| Low | Low | High | 262 | 274 |
| High | Low | Low | 294 | 315 |

From these figures it looks like slow hitting is worse than slow green clearance or slow movement. That is understandable since there are (in general) twice as many tee and fairway shots as greens to clear. But again the main point is that all of these runs involve all "fast" groups and the only reason the times are much higher than 4 hours is the variability. If we introduced "slow" players, the numbers jump even higher.

As in factory physics, variability is the enemy. Machine downtown, worker absenteeism, customer demand, raw material quality – any variation in those creates real problems for the plant manager. The same is true on the golf course. Variability is one of the factors creating the slow play problem.

In running simulations, the models replicate a day of activity. The figures displayed here show the average values for many (1,000 in most cases) days of play. Interestingly looking at one day at a time can be quite as instrumental as well as looking at the average of many days. When individual days are examined, great differences from one day to the next can be seen. Even when all things are "similar" such as having all fast players with some variability, there are days where things go smoothly by comparison and there are days when the time to play jumps way up. Some courses experience a regular, consistent pace, others good days and bad days. These can be explained by the random occurrence of some slow holes. Pin placements might slow some holes down. Even tee placements might make a difference. Most likely it is the random occurrence of a few groups having a bad day. Those few groups set the pace for everyone.

Below are two pictures of individual days from the same simulation. (Remember the figures presented earlier in this section are for runs of 1,000 days averaged together. These are two of those 1,000.) One day is good and the other is a problem. These are different only because of random events.

In the first day, the variability starts early causing even the first group to play in more than 4 hours. The pace of play increases gradually throughout the day and comes close to 5 hours by the end of the day.

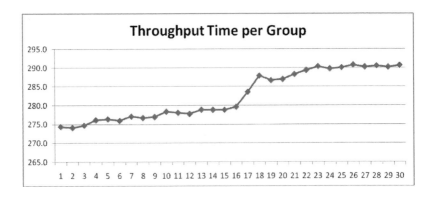

The total time each group waits for the whole round can be displayed as well. Here is that plot for the day displayed above:

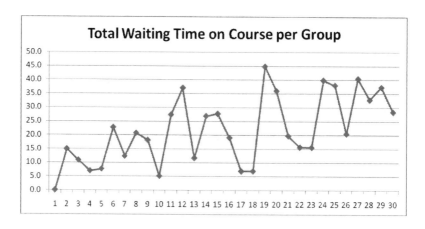

As can be seen, the amount of time a group waits varies greatly. Some groups wait very little – as little as 5 minutes – and others wait as much as 45 minutes. Some groups would leave the course that day and say that although the round took too long, it wasn't a bad day since they didn't wait very long. Other groups would say the day was miserable, not only did the round take too long but they had to wait on almost every shot. These runs explain the predicament of many course managers when they get such conflicting responses in the same day.

Here are the results for another day using the same basic information. Again these are all "fast" golfers with variability as described above. The pattern is somewhat different. The pace jumps quickly to a high level and stays there the rest of the day.

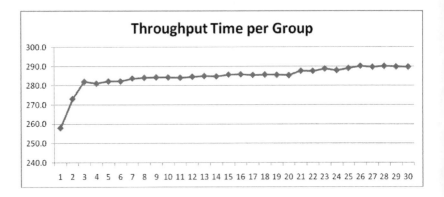

In this case although everyone played in essentially the same amount of time, again we see a large variation in the time each group waits. These are typical days in a course's life.

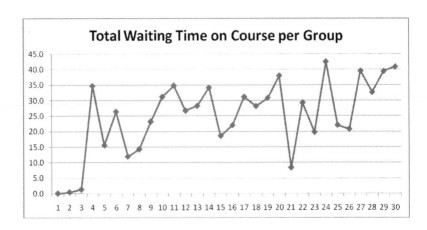

What is to be taken from this? It is that the problem is complex and it reveals itself to different parties in different ways. It has to be recognized that a multi-dimensional approach has to be taken to solve the problem.

These simulations are presented as examples of the work we have done to examine the complexity of the problem. What was presented here is not the full extent of the combinations tested. But there are quite representative and demonstrate a fairly rich examination of the subject. These were presented since they tell quite a story. They both illuminate as well as raise more questions.

To get a better understanding of the "Why" regarding waiting occurances, several closed-form stochastic models were created to find more general rules about pace of play. Some of those results are present in this next section.

## Where Is The Bottleneck?

One of the key indicators of a bottleneck operation is a pile of product waiting to be worked on (a full in-box in an office situation.) In Factory Physics terms, it is the operation which has a lot of WIP waiting to be worked on. In golf, par 3s are usually the place where groups pile-up. Factory Physics explains this. If the tee interval is shorter than the time it takes to play a par 3, a queue will appear at that par 3. But par

3s aren't the only place where golfers wait. Why is that?

Ward Whitt, my colleague at Columbia University, and his graduate student, Qi Fu, have developed a queueing model and an accompanying simulation model of golf holes and found the answer. Think of a par 4 hole as having three segments. The first is the segment in which the group tees off and then moves to the position where they can hit to the green (or believe they can hit to the green.) The next segment is the segment in which they actually do hit to the green. And the third segment is when they move to the green and then clear the green by finishing the hole and move on.

For par 4s, if the "time to tee off and walk to the place in the fairway where the shot to the green is to take place" (segment 1) takes less time than the "time to walk to the green after hitting the fairway approach shots plus the time to clear the green" (segment 3), there will be waiting time in the fairway. That can cause a backup all the way back to the tee. (The teeing ground is the only place where real queues with more than one group waiting can form.) On the other hand if the "tee and walk to fairway" time is greater than the "walk to and clear the green" time, then it is much less likely there will be waiting in the fairway. That is why some par 4s create waiting and others do not.

But another key element of Witt's study is that it is very easy for backups to occur if the green clearing time is large. Factory Physics is clear: you want the bottleneck to be near the front end of a process if possible rather than at the back end. For a hole you want the "tee to fairway" time to be higher than the "walk to and clear the green" time, or else you'll get backups on that hole. As such anything that can be done to get golfers to clear the greens quicker should lead to improved pace of play, whether that is slower green speeds, better hole placements, or "more efficient" putting such as giving short putts.

## The Nature of the Course

Except for the short discussion above and a mention that the first hole should be the bottleneck hole, very little has been mentioned here about the nature of the course itself. There are some things that can be done to the course to improve the pace. As mentioned above, pin and tee placements might make the course play harder or easier for groups to consistently play fast. The size of the fairway, the depth of the rough, the speed of the greens, and the placement of some trees might affect pace as well.

The course has several key effects on pace. First, the overall difficulty of the course can create many opportunities to play slowly. Lost balls, balls in the water, balls which can't be found in the rough all add time to a round. Each lost ball adds at least 5 minutes to a round, not just for that group but for just about every group behind. If several groups loose balls, each of those 5 minutes adds together. "Playing it Forward" is a good policy in most cases. But I contend golfers should not attempt even the front tees on many difficult courses. My rule is "do not play a course whose Slope Rating is more than 142 minus your Index." If you are a 10 handicap, look for a course with a set of tees with a Slope Rating in the mid 130's or less. For a 20 handicapper, look for one below 125. You can play a tougher course but you won't enjoy it and you'll just be slowing everyone else down.

The depth of the rough can cause missing a fairway to be almost as time consuming as a ball out of bounds. And I estimate (unscientifically) that each inch of green speed on the Stimpmeter above 10 adds between five and ten minutes to the round.

In addition to adding time, these things add imbalance. That means one group will play some holes (not necessarily all holes) more slowly than the group behind, thus not only slowing down the overall pace, but adding minutes to the total amount of "waiting for the group ahead to clear" time.

It just means more total waiting time in the round to hit your next shot. As was pointed out earlier, this actually may be a more frustration problem than the overall time.

So the nature of the course affects both the time to play and the time waiting for the group ahead to clear. It adds minutes and it adds variability. As was pointed out before, variability is our enemy. Courses have to be set up to reduce not increase golfer to golfer and group to group variability.

## Pace of Play, Tee Time Intervals

## and Revenue Maximization

One factor course management has control over is the tee time interval. As we saw earlier, our models clearly show that the pace of play and tee time intervals are closely related. For pace of play advocates, the argument against too small intervals is that rather than increasing revenue by putting more golfers on the course, small intervals result in slow play which not only discourages play but also actually reduces revenue by reducing the total number of groups who can play in a day. They are likely right on the first point, but are they right on the second point?

Kimes' simulations found a similar relationship between tee

interval and overall time to play in an effort to understand revenue maximization. The mathematical relationship they found took the shape of an exponential model. Taking their results and fitting them to a simple exponentiated model, we found that tee time interval and time to finish a round can be explained by the following formula:

Time to Play = 240 + (14 − Interval) ^ 2.7

where 240 minutes is the unimpeded time to play a round, and Interval is the Tee Time Interval in minutes.

Table 13

| Tee Time Interval | Time to Finish Round |
|---|---|
| 14 | 241 |
| 13 | 243 |
| 12 | 250 |
| 11 | 260 |
| 10 | 275 |
| 9 | 300 |
| 8 | 350 |
| 7 | 425 |

A tee time interval of 14 minutes would result in a 4 hour round. Anything less than that would add minutes to the round, just a few as it drops to 13 or 12 minutes but then a substantial amount as the interval drops below 9 minutes. In their model, at 8 minutes, the round will take close to 6 hours!

From the manager's perspective, short tee intervals mean management can push out more groups onto the course and therefore get more revenue. From a pace of play perspective the "optimal" time would be the shortest interval which does not lead to a substantial increase in pace. Is that the same "optimal" interval to maximize revenue?

Using the above model, a new formula was created to determine how many groups could be sent out in a 14 hour day and have all the groups complete their round. No consideration is given to "twilight rounds" or the possibility that the pace of play picks up as the sun starts to go down (queue dependent service times so to speak.) Both of those are very real but the assumption is that they are the same in all tested cases.

The number of groups that can be sent out in an hour can be found by dividing 60 minutes by the tee interval in minutes. If the interval was 10 minutes, six groups can be sent out. The shorter the interval, the higher the number of groups sent out. However the shorter the interval the longer the round and the fewer hours there'll be in the day for which all groups will complete the round. Therefore the number of groups who can complete a round of 18 holes in a day equals "the number of groups sent out per hour" times "the number of daylight hours in the day minus the time it takes to play all 18 holes." Combining those two relationships, we get:

$$\text{Number of Groups} = (60/\text{Interval}) * [14 \text{ hours} - (240 + (14 - \text{Interval})^{2.7})/60]$$

Total in Day

  where  Interval = Tee Time Interval

  14 Daylight Hours

  $240 + (14 - \text{Interval})^{2.7}$ calculates the time to play a round in minutes

This formula then yields the following total number of groups that can be sent out for each possible tee interval:

## Table 14

| Tee Time Interval | Total Number of Groups |
|:---:|:---:|
| 14 | 42.9 |
| 13 | 46.1 |
| 12 | 49.5 |
| 11 | 52.8 |
| 10 | 55.8 |
| 9 | 58.1 |
| **8** | **59.2** |
| 7 | 58.4 |
| 6 | 54.3 |

From these results it can be seen that using Kimes' results, the "optimal" revenue strategy for this course is to have an interval of 8 minutes. But that interval results in a 6 hour round! As such it is quite possible that in many cases, it is in management's best financial interests (at least in the short run) to have too short of a tee interval and "force" a 5, even a 6 hour round on their patrons. This poses a significant conundrum from a pace of play perspective.

To get a 4 hour round, the interval would have to increase to about 12 minutes. But that reduces the number of groups who can finish in a day by about 17%. Course owners are not going to do that unless they can raise prices 17% or, by reputation, get more golfers to play on those days that aren't filled. This is a serious obstacle to pace of play advocates.

If the course is full all the time, it is hard to argue for the pace of play point since the goal of any business is to maximize revenue. But if the course has trouble attracting players, then the longer tee intervals could be better.

Courses that are full may try longer intervals but raise their prices to compensate for the fewer (but happier) golfers. These trade-offs are a significant key to the problem.

# 7 THE PLAN: BRINGING BACK THE 4-HOUR ROUND

So what will it take to bring back the 4 hour round? What will it take to make that 4 hour round a maximum, not a minimum? Who has to be involved to get this done?

First let's be straight about 4 hours. It is by no means the absolute appropriate amount of time to play 18 holes of golf. For some courses and under some conditions more than four hours is appropriate. For other situations 3 hours might be appropriate. Think of 4 hours as a target, more like an attitude that we will not tolerate 5 or 6 hour rounds if they can be reasonably avoided.

Let me also point out, we are not talking about *speed* golf and we are not talking about rushing your play. We are not advocating running to your ball (although if you want to do that we won't stop you unless you are posing a real problem for other golfers on the course.) And we certainly don't want you to rush any shot which could lead to more slow play and less fun, i.e. a lost ball or a ball in the water etc.

So getting back to the question, how do we quicken the pace of play? Who has to be involved? The answer to this last question is, well, *everyone!* If you play golf, if you manage a golf course, if you design golf courses, if you run tournaments or club events, you are part of the problem, some more so than others. But we are all part of it, even if you are a "fast" player. But the research and experience provides the guidance on what has to be done.

I know you don't want to hear that. Everyone wants to think it is the other guy, the group ahead, or if not them the group ahead of them. Frank Thomas' surveys indicate that 70% of all golfers believe they are fast players. If that is true, why is play so slow?

Well, first, it's complicated. It's not just one thing. It's not just the players. It's not just the course set-up. It's not just the tee intervals. Simple answers won't do it. Slow play is the result of the interaction of many things. That's why we need a comprehensive Plan to get everyone involved, not just a gimmicky campaign. It is going to take hard work. (Who likes that – but that's the truth.)

The Plan has many dimensions, as many dimensions as the problem presents. It recognizes first, that everyone has a part to play, that this is a weakest link problem, that we have to stay on top of it or else we will go backwards, and most importantly that there is a hierarchy of things that must be done or else all other efforts are in vain.

First, tee intervals have to be set to match course and golfer characteristics to increase the chances that a 4 hour pace is possible. As golfers get better at pace of play behaviors, the interval can be shortened.

Second, course management has to understand the pace consequences of their course set up conditions, to monitor pace of play status at all times using modern technology, and reward "pace of play conscience" golfers.

Third, **all** golfers have to be instructed, trained, encouraged, and rewarded for moving directly to their own ball at a pace of at least 3 mph, hitting every shot in less than 45 seconds and getting their group to clear the green within 3 minutes *every time*.

Fourth, Ready Golf should be the standard for all

play and that some "adjustments" to the Rules may be in order. Reduce the time to look for a lost ball to 3 minutes. Eliminate the distance penalty for OB hits.

Each of the next four chapters explains these four steps.

# 8 TEE INTERVALS

As explained in Chapter 4, the golf course is like a factory. Goods are produced in a factory; foursomes are "produced" on a golf course. As such we have to be aware of the capacity of the bottlenecks in our "factory." In the factory if you try to make more product than the bottleneck can handle, work in process inventory builds up throughout the factory. The result is delays in several places and long throughput times. In our case that means long playing times.

So the first rule is that if you start more groups per hour than the bottleneck hole(s) can handle, you guarantee excessive round times. Most courses try to put as many groups on the course as possible to maximize revenue. But what they are doing is lengthening the round. They then love to point to the players themselves as being the problem when in fact they are the problem. This is the worst kind of management -

blaming the workers and not the process which management controls.

The par 3s tend to be the bottleneck holes. But other holes can cause backups as well. A short par 5 or a long par 4 could result in golfers waiting to hit even though they have little chance of reaching the green. Even short par 4s could cause problems since it takes less time to reach your fairway shots than it takes for the group ahead to clear the green. Management has to study every hole to see what the likelihood is that it will create backups. Assuming the par 3s are the bottleneck, the first two rules for management are:

- If it takes 10 minutes to play a par three and there is no waving up, then any tee interval less than 10 minutes essentially guarantees a long round no matter how conscientious the players are about fast play. An 8 minute tee interval almost certainly results in a 5 hour round on a reasonably difficult course.

- If the course allows groups to start as soon as the first fairway is open, they have guaranteed long rounds. This almost always puts too many groups on the course and although it may look good on the first hole, things back up quickly after that.

In some cases it can be more complicated than just matching the tee interval to the time it takes to play a par 3. In some cases a hole may not seem like a bottleneck but due to the high variability in the time it takes to play the hole, it can be the real problem hole. A medium length par 4 with lots of water or OB close to the fairway could create a high amount of variability. One group might play it fine and the next group might lose a ball or two. The difference in how long the different groups play the hole causes the kind of variability which leads to waiting on shots and slow play.

On the other hand the good news is that it might make sense to have short tee intervals for the first hour of the day. Since the course is empty at that time, the players who tee off first often see it as an opportunity to play quickly. In addition the early risers are often naturally faster players. So for the first hour, 8 minute tee intervals might work until the course is loaded. At some point as the course loads up, the tee interval can be increased to 9 minutes and then before noon they could be increased to the bottleneck cycle time of say 10 minutes.

**Before any education of individual golfers is considered, the course management has to do a study of its bottleneck hole(s) and establish a reasonable tee interval policy.**

Bill Yates has done this with Pebble Beach and has had big success. In these cases, *It Ain't the Players! It's the management!* A crowed highway of all Corvettes cannot go fast if there are too many vehicles on the road. It's not the cars or the drivers. That is obvious on the highways. Why is it not obvious on the golf course?

For a golf course to receive a Three/45 Golf Course ® designation, it has to demonstrate that it has done such a study, understands the relationship between tee intervals and bottleneck analysis, and has established and sticks to appropriate tee intervals.

In some cases this could lead to a loss of revenue. If the new tee interval leads to fewer groups going out in a day, that means less revenue for the course. However, in the long run, more golfers may want to play that course, perhaps even at a higher green fee. Or many might be willing to play at times the course's tee sheet previously had gaps. I am not against courses raising rates to maintain revenue if it is the result of a serious effort to reduce the time to play.

# 9 COURSE SET UP AND PACE MONITORING

One of my all-time favorite movies is Goldfinger. (My phone's ring tone is the James Bond theme.) Lots of shooting in that movie. No, I'm not referring to the guns. I mean lots of golf shots in that classic scene when Bond and Goldfinger played a match for a bar of gold. You may recall that the turning point in the match was the 17th hole when Goldfinger hit his drive into the left rough. As they looked for the ball, Odd Job dropped a new ball down his pant leg and declared it was Goldfinger's original ball. Of course it was not, because by that time, James had found the original but didn't let on, which set up the Rules sting on the 18th.

Why am I retelling this story? Simply this: Goldfinger didn't hit the ball in an impossible place. *He just hit it in the rough.* Why was it a problem to find a ball in the rough? My answer:

the rough was too high or too thick! If you hit a ball in the woods or bushes, looking for it can take some time. But it should never take 5 minutes to find a ball in the rough.

What does this have to do with pace of play? As pointed out in the research, every lost ball adds 5 minutes to the time it takes to play the hole. In some cases that time can be made up, but in most not. What if, as you are trying to make up that time, someone in the group ahead loses a ball? Now you're stuck.

How high or thick must the rough be to pose enough of a challenge to the average golfer to create a reasonable "penalty" for missing the fairway? My guess is if it is hard to find your ball in the rough, it is too high or thick. One inch, perhaps one and a half inches is enough of an obstacle for most golfers. Yes, it is ok that the US Open rough can be 3 or more inches of thick stuff, but every course?

My point is something as simple as the height of the rough may have a huge effect on pace of play. How about green speeds and hole placements? I would like to see a study done to test out one of my hypotheses: every inch of green speed on the Stimpmeter above 10 inches adds 5 to 10 minutes to the overall round time, and probably adds 15 to 30 additional total minutes of waiting to hit for all shots when added up.

Love those 3 and 4 putts!

"Playing it Forward" is a new program (although Frank Thomas and I proposed it in a 1980 USGA memo to eliminate the term "Ladies Tee") intended to help speed up play. Where should the forward tees be? To make Play it Forward work, the tees should be placed such that the high handicapper will not hit into trouble, such as fairway bunkers or small ponds or brooks. It might not work everywhere, but if it works anywhere, it is a good thing.

First, course management and superintendents should collect data on how long it takes to play each hole and where golfers are finding waiting times exorbitant. They should then test different strategies to see what works for pace without changing the fundamental balance of risk and reward for the typical golfer that day. If you are holding a championship, the course can be set up for expert golfers or for extra challenging conditions. But for every day play, the course should be set up to keep everyone moving in reasonable balance, yet still be challenging enough for players to enjoy the contest which makes the sport great.

Steve Southard's book [10] on course set-up is a must read for all course owners and superintendents. He is a clear thinker and a real practical person on the subject.

**As such, to be a Three/45 Golf Course ®, the superintendent should study how maintenance and set-up policies affect the pace at their course and implement actions to speed up play. Adjust the rough and greens speeds for the skill level of those typically playing the course and set the tee markers where hazards come less into play for high handicappers.**

Second, course management should know the status of pace of play at their course at all times. They should use the best technology available to know how today's play went, what the average time to play was by hour, where the problems were, what was the average group waiting time on the par 3 tees and other key points, which groups played quickly and which did not, plus other things of interest. You can't solve the problem without data. As was pointed out before, two groups could each play in a reasonable amount of time but one though it was fine and other thought it was painful.

You have to know the facts to understand what is really going on. Then this information has to be transmitted to the rangers so they can instruct golfers as to whether they are helping or hurting. Without accurate information, how can the rangers provide useful and accurate advice?

**Course management should implement, using advanced technology where possible, pace of play monitoring in real time so they know what is happening at any given time and to provide management information for future course set-up decisions.**

Third, the more information and feedback management gives to everyone involved can only lead to a better situation. At check in, players should receive the Three/45 Golf Pace of Play Principles ® to instruct them on what they should do to quicken the pace (see Chapter 10 for the Principles.) In addition, a pace rating schedule should be provided giving the group the times it should hit the check points on the course and how long the whole round should take. Management should post at least three check point signs on the course indicating how much time it should have taken to get to this point. The American Junior Golf Association is particularly good at this for their events. Why shouldn't every course use this every day?

**It is the responsibility of course management to provide as much information to the players as to what is acceptable behavior regarding pace of play. Time management estimates should be provided at check in**

**and on-course signs should indicate good performance.**

Fourth, each club or public/daily fee course should have a Pace of Play Chairman. Clubs currently have Green Chairman, Championship Chairmen, and Handicap Chairman. Why not a Pace Chairman who will be responsible for being sure everyone knows their contribution to the pace of play at that course? This person's job will be to educate and inform the members, the patrons about pace concerns and how each person can help. An on-the-scene person could make a big difference, if only by telling the world that this course takes the subject seriously.

**Each course/club should have a Pace of Play Committee with real leadership and real power to instruct and monitor pace of play.**

Lastly, recognize who the quicker players are. Reward them in as many ways as you can. Early tee times, a free soda or beer after the round, a hat for the quickest round of the day starting after 10 am.

**A Three/45 Golf Course reinforces a quicker pace of play by identifying and rewarding good pace of play behaviors.**

For example, why can't courses give preferred tee times to

"fast/low variability" golfers? This author proposed in his 1987 Golf Digest article that each golfer should have a pace of play handicap. Bill Williams (when he was president of the USGA) suggested that fast players be rewarded with the first tee times of the day. The models confirm that sequencing golfers from fast to slow would improve the pace significantly. Of course the models also show that even "fast" players who exhibit too much variability will hurt this strategy, so the pace will still have to be monitored.

It should be pointed out, however, that some people may not want to play very fast. Perhaps they are just learning the game. Of course the proper pace related behaviors have to be learned as well. But the course may set aside some "relaxed" tee times for people who are just not capable of playing quickly. Like flashing lights on a slow moving truck, these people could be identified, given appropriate tee times, and be instructed to wave through faster groups.

There is an art to waving through a group. In some cases they can play along with the passing group as long as it doesn't endanger anyone or create an annoyance. The objective is to get out of the way of the group coming through, but if the slow players just stop thinking about what to do next, the slow group will perpetually be waiting. There may be another group right behind the passing group ready to come through as well. If that is the case, the slow group shouldn't be on the course at that time, or should make a serious effort to pick up the pace.

**A Three/45 Golf Course ® encourages slow groups to wave through quicker groups if their intention is to play slowly. Otherwise the slow group has to be instructed in the Pace of Play Principles ® so they can learn to play at an appropriate pace.**

# 10 INDIVIDUAL PLAYER AND GROUP BEHAVIORS

Sam Sneed said that if you are playing poker and you don't know who the pigeon is, guess what? You're the pigeon. If you don't know who is causing the slow play, it is likely you!

As said earlier, almost all of the discussion about what cause slow play has focused on individual and group behaviors. As this book has pointed out, we really can't even discuss this part of the problem until Tee Intervals are set appropriately and course set-ups are done with pace of play in mind and pace monitoring is done seriously. If those things aren't done first, almost nothing that follows will have any effect. Have I made myself clear?

Having said that, there is no question that poor pace of play behaviors by individuals and groups as a whole lead to long playing times and worse, lots of waiting on individual shots for the group ahead to clear.

Good, so now we can talk about player and group behaviors. What can be said which hasn't already been said? I pointed out in Chapter 5 that Pat Mateer wrote probably the clearest book on the subject of individual behaviors which affect pace of play, the good and the bad. His book is out of print (I hope to change that) because he got frustrated that people weren't paying attention. He was right to get frustrated. People just were not focusing on this issue at that time. But things have changes somewhat and now we have a chance to make real progress and his ideas and prose should live on.

His book says there are four rules players should follow. They are *Be Prepared, Be in Position, Simplify Your Routines and Move with Purpose.* In essence he is saying move directly to your own ball and immediately begin preparing for your next shot so that you are ready to hit in a short time after it is your turn. It is sound advice.

As demonstrated in Chapter 6, my research (and that of others) has led me to create the following Principles:

## The Three/45 Golf Pace of Play Principles ©

Principles for Individuals:

1. Walk **directly to your own ball** at a speed of at least **3 MPH** (about 100 yards a minute.)
2. Be ready to hit and never take more than **45 seconds** to plan, address and hit a shot (average far less.) Start preparing your stroke as soon as you arrive at your ball even while others are hitting.
3. Never take more than **3 minutes** to look for a lost ball or a ball in the water.
4. Pick up or concede putts when you are **3 strokes** out of the hole.
5. Read a good book such as The Return of the Four Hour Round by Pat Mateer at least **3** times
6. Teach the Principles to at least **3 new players** each time you go to the course.
7. Share at least **3 pace of play** ideas, known successes and failures with the Three/45 Web Social Site.
8. Organize a **Three/45** club in your area to advocate for a quicker pace of play.

Principles for Groups:

1. Your group should never take more than **3 minutes** to clear the tee, fairway landing area or green.
2. Limit the **number** of players looking for lost balls to **3** – the fourth should be hitting.
3. Wave up the following group on **Par 3s** if a group is waiting before you have reached the green.

4. If your group is out of position, speed up and get back in position within **3 strokes.**

Clyne Soley, a USGA volunteer researcher, was doing golf analytics before Bill James was born. He was a very quick playing, single digit handicapper in his younger days but as he got old, he rarely scored better than 90. Did he slow down? Not at all! He would move directly to his ball and have the shot figured out almost before he got to his ball. I used to joke that taking the club out of his bag was part of his back swing. As far as I am concerned, he was the ideal golfer.

Bill Bradley was a great NBA star with the Knicks. His key to success was "movement without the ball." He would get himself into position while everyone was watching the ball handler, and then one good pass (from Clyde or Phil Jackson) gave him an open shot which he almost always made. Wayne Gretsky, likewise, credited his movement without the puck for his great scoring success. In golf what you do when it is not your turn can make all the difference between a 4 hour and a 5 hour round.

Golfers should always be ready to hit once it is their turn everywhere on the course, but on the putting greens, this behavior is crucial. While others are putting, get your line and green speed figured out so that when it is your turn you can move right into your set up. And if you miss the putt (God forbid), watch it go past the hole so you can see the line and not have to start all over to figure out what you are going to do. Clearing the green in 3 minutes is an absolute must to get the overall pace back in order.

The models when run with a 3 mph pace, taking an average of 30 seconds to hit and no more than 3 minutes to clear the tee, fairway and green, everyone plays in 4 hours or less even with a modest amount of variability. Together these factors will create an environment (a factory) which can be receptive to fast play and to golfers who would now be capable of playing quickly. All of these factors, when put into the models, lead to the creation of 4 hour rounds.

**The Three/45 Golfer ® follows the Pace of Play Principles ® and helps others to do the same. He/she is an advocate and a leader.**

Theoretically there is no reason that we can't play in 3 hours. As crazy as that might seem, it is not only possible but some people regularly do it. Think about it. In an 18 hole round, a typical golfer walks 4 miles. At 3 mph that's 80 minutes of walking. If a golfer takes 100 strokes to complete the round and no stroke takes more than 45 seconds (not too terribly fast), that's another 75 minutes. The total of those two is 155 minutes, just over 2 and one half hours! So why does it take so long to play? All the rest of the time is spent waiting. Waiting for the group ahead to clear, waiting for others in your group to play, waiting to find a ball, etc. Although waiting for others in your group is sometimes necessary (like on the tee or green), it can be minimized. Some things can be done simultaneously, especially for shots in the fairway. Play Ready Golf whenever you can, and "give" putts when they don't really matter.

Lastly, if you do follow these Principles ® yet still wait on some shots, do not get frustrated, do not get discouraged, do not get angry, and absolutely do not abandon the Principles ®. Waiting on some shots is not only inevitable, but may occur because everyone is trying to move more quickly. Since we all can't move at the exact same pace, some congestion will happen.

One of the facts that came from my simulations of Pace of Play was that even if the overall pace was quick, there would be times when your group will have to wait on a shot. That is because not everyone and every group play at the same pace on every hole. Even if all groups were trying their best to maintain a quick pace, there will be times when a group loses a ball, or a ball goes in the water and a discussion about a drop ensues, or a difficult green or pin placement creates some three putts.

This kind of variability creates waits even when everyone is trying to be good. In Factory Physics, variability is the enemy (I tell my students.) The same is true on the golf course. Because of this variability, you may get behind. But you may also bunch up. It is ok to catch up to the group ahead. In a situation where overall time to play may be improving, there may be some slight increases in waiting to hit situations. It is all part of the progress to a better overall time to play.

Some courses are more prone to variability problems. Some golfers are more prone to create them. You will notice that the Three/45 Pace of Play Principles © make mention in several places on how to reduce variability by never taking more than 3 minutes to look for a lost ball (although the Rules allow 5), by never taking more than 45 seconds to hit (although you should average far less), by clearing the tee, fairway and green in 3 minutes, and by encouraging managers to set up their courses to minimize playing "crashes" like the lost ball or three putt.

But even with all of those and with everyone following the Principles ©, some waiting will occur. Actually my simulations show that even with a modest amount of hole by hole and group by group variability, every group will wait some amount, and that total wait time will vary from group to group and possibly by a large amount. So there could be a day when everyone plays in 4 hours but one group had to wait on several shots and another group not often at all. The group that waited a fair amount on their shots might complain that it was a "slow" day while the other group said it was a great day because they almost never waited to hit. Although both played in 4 hours, their experience was different.

The gist of this is we need to remember that just by getting the total time to play down under 4 hours, we still need to recognize that there will be some waiting due to the imbalance of the time to play each hole by each group. So we need to keep a couple of points in mind beyond the Principles ©. The Principles © tell us what **TO** do. But we also need Principles © of what **NOT** to do. Here is a start. Please suggest more:

1. Never get frustrated by the Pace. Keep your head in your game.
2. Never give up on the Principles © or on teaching them to other golfers and course managers.
3. Never get angry with the group ahead. They may not be the problem even if they are not playing by the Principles ©. Always remain courteous.

4. Never rush your swing. A bad shot does more to slow down play than the time you think you might save.

The Three/45 Golf Association is not about Speed Golf. Speed Golf may be a fun thing, but it is not for everyone. We want a quicker pace of play, but we don't want people to rush or think everyone can play as quickly as everyone else. We also don't believe that we can eliminate all waiting. Actually as we get quicker, we may create some inadvertent waiting because we caught up to the group ahead so quickly. Some waiting time may be more indicative of our good pace, not their bad pace. And although we love your passion for advocating for a quicker pace of play, let's always keep in mind we are all here for the enjoyment of the game.

What we are trying to do is get the overall pace to a reasonable time, for most courses, under 4 hours, maybe even down to 3:45! But we want the experience of playing to be as pleasant and as enjoyable as possible for everyone.

# 11 SOME ADJUSTMENTS TO THE RULES

The Rules are great. We need the USGA Rules to be the governing principles for our play. But the Rules are anything but cast in stone. They are a work in progress. I hope the USGA will look at some of its Rules and adjust them to help with pace issues.

The first is the 5 minutes to look for a lost ball. The Rules don't stop you from taking less time than 5 minutes. That doesn't break the Rules. So I recommend cutting off the search at 3 minutes. I think that should be the standard, especially if courses smarten up and reduce the height of the rough!

What if the ball is indeed lost? The Rules require you to go back and play a new stroke from where the last one was taken or to play on with a provisional ball if appropriate and if one was first played. Both cases add plenty of time. Why not use a modified water hazard rule for casual rounds? If lost, add a stroke but don't lose the distance. Don't hit a provisional. Instead, invoke this modification. That would save lots of time. (Many people already use this rule for their casual play. Why? Because it make sense and speeds up play. The league I play in uses this rule and it works.)

"Inside the leather" is an old saying seldom heard these days, possibly because of the long putters, inside the leather may be 5 feet today! But "giving" putts of short length in casual rounds is a good idea. Why because it is likely that the major source of slow play in many cases can be found on the greens. If the greens are bottlenecks, the whole hole will back up. Let's clear the green within 3 minutes.

I'm sure there are other Rules which should be looked at. The Rules are too complicated to begin with and discussions about how to comply with them could add a chunk of time to the round.

# 12 IMPLEMENTING "THE PLAN"

Everything is in place. All the information we need is available. So what's the Plan? First get course management, PGA professionals, and superintendents on board. Second get as many golfers as possible to become Three/45 Golfers ®.

First we need to get course management totally committed to having an appropriate pace of play policy. Course management has to take the lead. The players cannot do it themselves. This is a weakest link problem from the players' standpoint. Getting some or even most golfers interested is not enough if too many "slow" players remain. It's not how many we educate; it's how many remain ignorant or oblivious. Someone has to exert leadership. The course is the most appropriate place to start.

A pace-conscience course should follow the Three/45 Golf Association Course Guidelines ® and become a certified Three/45 Course ®. To be certified, a course should register on the www.three45golf.org web site and demonstrate they follow the minimum guidelines below. Once registered, they should proudly indicate to all golfers their status as a course actively trying to improve the pace of play.

**The Three/45 Pace of Play Improvement Plan Guidelines ® are:**

- **Determine an appropriate tee interval policy with pace of play as the most significant factor in making that policy.**

- **Establish appropriate course set-up conditions which enhance pace efforts rather than pose pace problems**

- **Institute modern pace monitoring procedures including using advanced communications technology and providing feedback to players, rangers and clubhouse management**

- Provide pace instruction and pace rating material at check in and prominently post the Three/45 Golf Pace of Play Principles ®.

- Encourage Three/45 Golf Association membership to all players. Create Pace of Play Committees and Chairmen at every course.

- Provide rewards to players and groups who make a serious effort to be part of the solution

A course which puts this part of the Plan into effect has done all golfers a great service and has significantly advanced the pace of play movement. Individual golfers should sign up for the Three/45 Golf Association and play by the Three/45 Pace of Play Principles for Individuals and Groups ®. Golfers should form local Three/45 clubs to reinforce the Principles ® and to encourage others to join in. Club/course PGA pros could lead them in Pace instruction as well as game improvement instruction. Everyone should be encouraged to seek out new information such as the educational material the USGA is providing and the

Three/45 Golf Association provides as to what works and what doesn't. Local efforts to improve pace should then be shared so such efforts can be implemented elsewhere. In other words we all need to help each other, and by doing so we will all be better off.

## The Role of Psychology/the Role of Leadership

I've always enjoyed playing in the evening after work. To finish the 18th as the dusk begins to dominate the sky on a warm summer evening is a real pleasure for me. And often while doing that I noticed that a slow group ahead of me all of a sudden would begin to pick up the pace as the sun started to go down and the chance of not finishing the whole round became a real possibility. I, being young and foolish, would inappropriately yell at them, "why didn't you play at this pace all *!/+* round?"

I didn't make many friends doing that. But of course it was true. People can play faster than they currently mostly do. How do we get them to do that?

Behavioral research is still not a perfect science, but some insights have been discovered over the years. One of the most significant is that people will do the right thing if you tell them what the right thing is. Second they are more likely to do the right thing if you tell them why it is the right thing.

Third they are more likely to do the right thing if they are told most people do the right thing and actually see people doing the right thing. The right thing here is to play by the Three/45 Golf Pace of Play Principles ® and to get the course management to become leaders in the movement.

A corollary to that is telling golfers what not to do is not nearly as helpful as telling them what to do. If you have kids, you know that telling them "not to do something" rarely works. They do not hear the NOT. They just hear the action, and most likely continue doing exactly what you don't want them to do. Leadership is getting people to do what is right. Let's be leaders by explaining what actions lead to a quicker pace, rather than telling golfers what not to do.

I have a rule: never tell a stupid person they are stupid, because after you have done that, you are now dealing with an *angry* stupid person. In this case, never tell a slow golfer they are slow. Tell them they should pick up the pace and explain what they should do (follow the Principles ®.)

Providing feedback is a smart way to encourage golfers to consider pace issues. At several courses, Brooklawn Country Club in Connecticut and South Hills in Southern California to name two, post group playing times. In both cases average round times are under 4 hours. Something as simple as that may be enough in some places to make a big difference, especially if the club has implemented the other aspects of the plan, such as appropriate tee intervals and sound course set ups.

Pat Mateer has even told me when he implemented some pace of play improvements at the Taylor Made Invitational (a handicap amateur event), the pace quickened by 50 minutes, and average scores improved a stroke. You can play better by playing quicker.

One of the missions of the Three/45 Golf Association is to create a legion of golfers who know what the right things to do are and to have them provide the visual and vocal leadership needed to get everyone on the same page.

Remember this is a weakest link problem. If we get some golfers on board, that is likely not enough. We need to get a critical mass before we will see real progress. We need to get course managers, superintendents and club/course PGA pros on board as well. But fundamentally we need to teach people by example. That is the truest form of leadership. Let's stick to our principles. Others will follow and in turn become new leaders.

## The Call to Arms

The Plan, to be successful, must reach out to everyone.

- We need to get **every golf club/course** certified as a Three/45 Golf Course or Club ®.

- We need to get **every superintendent** to understand the effect their work has on pace.

- We need **every golfer** to be aware of how their behaviors and their group behaviors affect the pace of play.

The first is critical. We have to start with the courses and clubs. It is the courses/clubs which have to take the initial lead before the individual golfers can make a difference. So to get the clubs and courses involved, I call on the PGA of America, the USGA, the Golf Superintendents Association, the Golf Architects Association, the National Golf Foundation, and every other national organization to reach out to every course and every club in their sphere of influence with the Three/45 Plan ® and ask them to get on board.

The USGA is already doing its part as the leaders of the game, a role they have performed magnificently for over 100 years. And although they don't like to be called the "rulers of the game," they really are just that. They should be proud of the terrific job they have done in providing leadership on all critical issues affecting the game: on the Rules, on course conditions, on equipment, on handicapping and now on pace.

I believe the club pros of the PGA of America are the "heart and soul" of the game. They are on the front lines of being sure that the best interests of the game are maintained on its "playing field." They have great power to influence progress on pace.

The course superintendents simply are the "backbone" of the game. It is their hard work which makes the environment as enjoyable as it is, a significant attraction which should not be under appreciated. But if they go about their work without understanding the pace of play consequences of the choices they make, much of their great work goes in vain.

The designers of courses are, of course, the true artists in this industry. It is their work which determines if the land will "speak" to the golfers and draw them back again and again.

The National Golf Foundation represents the best interests in all of those people who provide the tools and inspiration to make the game enjoyable. Their work helps many aspects of the game by encouraging participation and growth.

All of these organizations must reach out (as the USGA has done already) to all its members to get the message that we must solve this problem. Not just any one group, but everyone together.

If all clubs would establish a Pace of Play Chairperson, and if every public and daily fee course would follow the Guidelines ® and then disseminate the Pace of Play Principles ® to every golfer as they check in, we can raise the level of awareness and see real improvement.

# 13 THE FUTURE

Why is one factory productive and another not? Although the workers are usually blamed, most often it is a combination of factors. Often it is the set-up of the factory itself, the processes, the machines, the materials that the workers have to contend with. Sometimes the workers haven't been trained properly and don't know they are doing things wrongly. Sometime it is management not taking charge. In the golf course as factory, we have all of these. Someone has to take charge of this issue and improve each of the factors. The Plan is designed to recognize all of those factors and put in place the actions needed to make this a more enjoyable game.

- Individual golfers have to recognize how they contribute to slow play. They have to learn the behaviors which will help quicken the pace of play. Becoming a Three/45 Golf member and following the Principles of Pace of Play ® is a good start.

- Superintendents have to understand the specifics of the pace problem they face and set up their courses recognizing those issues. Rough height, green speeds, tee and hole placements and fairway widths all have pace contribution which has to be understood and adjusted.

- Managers have to decide whether they want a tee interval that guarantees a 5 hour round, or to choose an interval that gives the golfing public a chance at a decent pace of play. Without an appropriate tee interval, all else is naught.

The information needed to "pick up the pace" now exists. This book presents a Plan to get it done. We just need the will. Join the Three/45 Golf Association. Get your course certified as a Three/45 Golf Course ® . Ask your PGA Professional to become as much of an expert in pace as he or she is about the golf swing. Form a Three/45 Golf Club to teach others the Principles ® and the Plan ®. Be part of the movement for a quicker pace of play.

# CONCLUDING UNSCIENTIFIC POSTSCRIPTS

Abraham Lincoln once said "he who has the right to criticize, has the heart to help." If you find anyone who is critical of the pace of play at their course, ask them to join in the movement by becoming a Three/45 Golfer ®. Tell them to become member of the Three/45 Golf Association and be a leader and not a complainer. We need to get everyone involved. We need everyone to be positive about their contribution. I hope this book is an inspiration to all golfers to help in this effort.

This is the first edition of the book and I want to improve it. Please send your ideas and comments so we can make real progress. Send them to the Three/45 Golf Association web site, www.three45golf.org.

# REFERENCES

1. National Golf Foundation, Jupiter, Florida
2. Growing The Game, Frank Thomas, Frankly Golf Consulting LLC, 2005
3. "What Is Your Fast Play Handicap?", Lucius Riccio, Golf Digest July 1987
4. The Return of The Four HourRound, Pat Mateer
5. Factory Physics, Mark Spearman, McGraw-Hill/Irwin Series Operations and Decision Sciences (2000)
6. "Golf Course Revenue Management: A Study of Tee Time Intervals", Sherly Kines and Lee Schruben, Journal of Revenue and Pricing Management, Vol 1 No 2 (2002)
7. "Daily Play at A Golf Course: Using Spreadsheet Simulation to identify System Constraints", Andrew Tiger and Dave Salzer, INFORMS Transactions on Education, Vol 4 No 2 (2004)
8. Yates, B. (2011) Get A Move On. LINKS Magazine. Retrieved from www.linksmagazine.com/best_of_golf/get-a-move-on.
9. "USGA Pace Rating System", USGA. Golf House, Far Hills, New Jersey
10. Southard, Steve, Mastering Pace of Play While Maximizing Revenue, 2010

# ACKNOWLEDGEMENTS

I would like to thank Frank Thomas (inventor of the graphite shaft, and the use of the Stimpmeter for green speeds and the creator of the USGA Equipment Test Center) and Pat Mateer (The Return of the Four Hour Round) for their reading of the manuscript and for their help formulating the ideas which led to this book. I want to thank my colleague Mark Broadie who almost forcefully encouraged me to publish the work I was doing on pace of play.

Jay Mottola, executive direct of the Metropolitan Golf Association has given me the opportunity to write about pace on more than one occasion. His support has been critical in getting the message out. Jerry Tarde, Golf Digest editor, helped me produce my first article on pace in 1987 which really was the beginning for me.

Several Columbia University students over a several year period helped build the models discussed in this book. Several of these models served as the basis of the science behind the "Plan."

I would like to thank Chip Armstrong, Jon Silverberg, Mike Weiss and Vikram Joshi for their help in the creation of the Three/45 Golf Association. Casey Alexander of the Nassau Players Club gave me course maintenance suggestions of real importance. And lastly my heartfelt thanks to Laura Shanley for her patient and meticulous help in getting this book in shape for printing, something I could never have done on my own.

# ABOUT THE AUTHOR

For over 30 years, **Lucius J. Riccio**, (a.k.a. "the Pope of Pace"), the founder of the Three/45 Golf Association, has been active in the administration and improvement of the game of golf. He has studied golf related issues using his statistical and analytical skills learned while earning three engineering degrees including a Ph.D. from Lehigh University.

His early golf work included two research proposals and data analysis projects in the 1970's which, in part, lead to the development of the USGA Slope System. As an original member of the USGA's Handicap Research Team and as a member of its Handicap Procedure Committee, he has served that organization for over 30 years and is the recipient of the USGA's prestigious Isaac Grainger Award.

In 1977, he developed the game's first complete statistical recording system (which he offered to the PGA Tour.) Using that system, he was the first to develop and market personal computer based software (the Golf Analyzer ®) to analyze an individual golfer's game and has used it to study the play of hundreds of golfers including major championship winners Arnold Palmer, Jack Nicklaus, Tom Watson and Sherri Steinhauer as well as amateurs of all levels of play.

He has worked on golf course development projects, of most note for Donald Trump on the creation of some of his finest golf course projects. In addition Mr. Riccio is a member of the team that manages the Parks Department's Silver Lake Golf Course on Staten Island and Marine Park Golf Course in Brooklyn, whose playing condition has been upgraded to near country club quality.

He has served on the Executive Committee of the Metropolitan (NY) Golf Association and the MGA Foundation Board of Directors. He serves as a tournament rules official, having passed the USGA Rules Test after learning the Rules while riding New York's subways to and from work.

He currently is a Professional Advisor for Golf Digest and a regular statistical contributor to that magazine. Over the last three decades, he has had many articles published in Golf Digest, Golf Magazine, Senior Golfer and The Met Golfer magazines. He also has written chapters in golf books, most notably a chapter in Johnny Miller's book **Breaking 90.**

In his golfing life, his handicap index ranged in the high single digits until age has taken its toll. He credits his own statistical analyses as being instrumental in achieving the single-digit level. One of his greatest achievements in golf was winning the 1989 NYC Department of Sanitation Golf Tournament at Split Rock Golf Course against arguably the "strongest" field in golf.

In 2013, Mr. Riccio was awarded the Inaugural ShotLink® Intelligence Prize by the PGA Tour for his paper "The Best Ball Striker on Tour", for which Columbia University received a $25,000 CDW Technology Grant.

Mr. Riccio is on the faculty of Columbia University and teaches Business Analytics in its Business School, Engineering College and School of International and Public Affairs. He is the head of Columbia University's Consortium for Advanced Sports Analytics. In addition he is the Executive Vice President of Gedeon GRC, a New York based full service engineering firm, and is a Registered Professional Engineer in the State of New York.

Made in the USA
Coppell, TX
22 February 2024

29321030R00072